MRS. ANNIE BESANT
A Psychological Study

MRS. ANNIE BESANT
A Psychological Study

BEPIN CHANDRA PAL

GYAN

Published by

Gyan Publishing House
5, Ansari Road
Daryaganj, New Delhi-110002
Phone: 011-47034999, 9811692060
E-mail: books@gyanbooks.com

Distribution Network
gyanbooks.com
India, USA, Canada, UK, Australia, France

ISBN : 978-81-212-8228-4 (PB)
First Published, 1917

2nd Impression 2024

Printed at: Gyan Press, Delhi.

MRS. ANNIE BESANT
A Psychological Study
Author: BEPIN CHANDRA PAL

Contents

APOLOGIA 9

MRS. ANNIE BESANT A CHARACTER SKETCH 11

MRS. BESANT'S BRAHMACHARYA 15

THE PSYCHIC PLANE AND THE SPIRITUAL PLANE 16

MRS. BESANT'S SELF-CENTREDNESS 21

PSYCHOLOGY OF MRS. BESANT'S CONVERSION 26

MRS. BESANT'S CONTRIBUTIONS TO THEOSOPHY 32

MRS. BESANT'S CONTRIBUTIONS TO THE HINDU REVIVAL 34

MRS. BESANT'S YOUTHFUL SECULARISM 38

FROM ATHEISM TO AGNOSTICISM 43

MRS. BESANT'S MISSIONARY METHODS 66

IN THE SERVICE OF FREEDOM 99

AGAINST LAWLESSNESS AND CRIMINALISM 118

MRS. BESANT'S POLITICAL PRINCIPLES AND METHODS 125

BENGAL NATIONALISM AND MRS. BESANT 127

TOWARDS A UNITED CONGRESS 143

CORRECTIONS 160

What is Prayer

Who pants and struggles to be free
Who strives for others' liberty
Who failing, still works patiently
He truly prays.

Who, loving all, dare none despise
But with the worst can sympathise
Who for a truth a martyr dies
He truly prays

Who, when a truth to him is known
Embraces it through smile or frown
Who dares to hold it, though alone
He truly prays.

In musing strength must come to
Petitions are but empty air [dare
Brave action is the only prayer
Thus learn to pray.

—Annie Besant.

"It is better to suffer than to consent to, wrong. It is better to lose liberty than to lose honour. I am old, but I believe that I shall see India win Home Rule before I die. If I have helped ever so little to the realisation of that glorious hope I am more than satisfied"

—Annie Besant

APOLOGIA

This book is not at all what I should have liked to make it. Part of it is a reprint of a Character-Sketch published in the *Hindu Review.* The original idea of the Publishers was to reprint that Sketch with a few additional pages dealing with Mrs. Besant's political activities.

They made this offer to me before Mrs. Besant's internment. Before, however, I sat down to write the "additions," news flashed that she had been deprived of her freedom by the Government of Madras.

This changed all my plans; and the Publishers also had to revise their original plan and estimate in consequence of it.

I could not allow an old and scrappy Sketch to go out to the public now. But when I resolved to revise and re-write the whole thing, I found that the earlier Sketch had already been set up and partly struck off. I had no opportunity of looking over the proofs. The Publishers were naturally in a hurry to get the book out as soon as possible. And I had to write and post the new matter also from day to day without being able to examine the book as a whole, and to re-adjust the different parts in the light of this whole, before it was placed with the printers.

This accounts for the loose structure of the book as between the earlier and the latter parts of it.

The Character-Sketch of Mrs. Besant published in 1913, and reprinted in the first few pages, of this book, was based upon my *impressions* of her life and writings. I remember to have read her Auto-biography, or extracts from it, more than twenty years ago. Having been connected with public life and journalism ever since I was a youth of eighteen or nineteen, I had followed Mrs. Besant's career almost from the day when she came to be widely known as an Atheist and a Freethinker. I had read of her conversion to Theosophy as a contemporary event, and had heard her lecture in Calcutta when she first came here; and had known of her propagandist work ever since. The Sketch in the Hindu Review was based upon the accumulated impressions gathered through all these years. They were, however, outside impressions only. I had not as yet the privilege of personal acquaintance with her. I had tried to study her, therefore, through the intellect only. And though I tried to be just and appreciative, I must confess that in 1913, I had not that sympathy with her without which the deeper chambers of our true soul and character can never be opened.

Since then, I have met her; and, what is more, have, in my humble way, been a co-worker with her in a common cause. This kinship has revealed to me today the inner soul of this great Fighter for Truth and Freedom, more intimately than before.

Mrs. Besant is a born rebel. I too am one, in my humbler way. She has passed through doubt and denial, religious excommunication and social ostracism; so have I. She has found a larger faith gradually; God has not withheld it from me. She has found her Master. The Master has graciously claimed me also. And we share a common political faith today, described as Nationalist Imperialism by our common friend Mr. W. T. Stead. I am not a Theosophist, in the present technical sense of the term. But, I can, perhaps, claim a community of make and experience with Mrs. Besant, more intimate than most of her Theosophic followers. Sitting down to study her life and character today, not "Critically" as I did before, but with sympathy and affection, I have discovered the truth of it more clearly than I had done in 1913, when the sketch in the *Hindu Review* was published.

The right of printing and publishing this book in India is vested in Messrs. Ganesh & Co., for five years from August, 1917. The right of translation, and republication in foreign lands is reserved to me.

August 10th, 1917 **BEPIN CHANDRA PAL**

Bhowanipur, Calcutta

OM
Mrs. ANNIE BESANT
A CHARACTER SKETCH

Though not of our country by birth, nor of our people by race, Mrs. Besant has been, for more than a quarter of a century, one of the most prominent figures in our public life. And to-day, there is, perhaps, not another person, in any Indian province, to whom the heart of awakened India goes with greater reverence and deeper affection than it does to this strange woman from beyond the seas.

A magnetic personality, a finished orator, a capable organiser, endowed with large powers of imagination and sympathy, and with a very rare combination of the subtle wisdom of the diplomat with the fervour of the prophet, Mrs. Besant's influence over a very large section of our English-educated countrymen has been hardly less than that of any other leader of thought in India of the present generation.

In the earlier years of her consecrated service to India, she very materially helped to wean away the sympathies of good many English-educated Indians, especially in the South, from the so-called free-thought and secularism of the middle-nineteenth-century European culture, and very largely rehabilitated for them the faith and philosophy of their fathers. In her latest activities she has been a most powerful influence to wean away good many people from separatist ideals of isolated sovereign national independence, and draw them to the higher ideal of federated and co-operative internationalism, in and through which, every Empire must find its only ethical justification, as well as its highest social and spiritual self-fulfilment, as a mediating step in social Evolution, between Nationalism and Universal Humanity.

English education and the conflict of ideals which it created had well-nigh killed not only the faith of large and increasing numbers of our educated middle class in the beliefs and traditions of their race, but had commenced to turn away many of them, especially in Madras, into rank atheists and "free-thinkers." Owing to the influence of the Brahmo Samaj, and to some extent of the Arya Samaj also, this so-called free-thought was not so rampant in Northern India as it was in the Southern Presidency. But neither Keshub Chunder nor Day-ananda, neither Ranade nor any one else could have stemmed the tide of this so-called free-thought and secularism, so far as this large class of people were concerned, so successfully as Mrs. Besant has undoubtedly done. Hidebound Hindu orthodoxy may not have been seriously affected by her apolegetics and exegetics, which did not always follow the lines of the ancient exegetical literature of our race. Her readings of Hindu philosophy and her interpretations of Hindu rituals, may have seemed to some as a medley of modern scepticism and ancient supernaturalism. But notwithstanding all this, one cannot reasonably refuse to acknowledge the immense debt that the present generation of English-educated Hindus owe to her. One may question the validity of her spiritual claims. One may not accept her science as true or her philosophy as sound. There may be,—indeed, there are— the widest possible difference of opinion in the country about these matters. But no one, I think, can refuse to admit the very patent fact that large numbers of our educated countrymen, especially in wife whose husband has no element of the unknown, and the mysterious in him. The teacher who is a *mere man* to his disciple, can exercise but little influence over him. Modern rationalism, by killing this sense of the unknown and the mysterious in us practically destroys the very plinth and foundations of our spiritual life. The leader who is not a bit of a mystery to his following can rarely lead them to any superior achievement. We all know the air of mystery that always hung over Napolean.

It is, indeed, the common characteristic of all those, whether men or women, who have any pretentions to what, in the philosophy of Bernard Shaw, would be called superman-hood. The superman is always a character. And a character is always a complexity and a mystery. He who runs may never read the man or woman of character. They are always a strange medley of apparent contradictions. And it is through these very contradictions that they exercise such fascinating influence over their fellow-beings. Mrs. Besant is a character, a bit of a mystery, a medley of contradictions, and an interesting psychological problem. And this has been, I think, her most valuable asset in life.

MRS. BESANT'S PHYSICAL ENDOWMENTS

Love of abstraction has been so dominant a feature of the culture and education of the nineteenth century, that few people seem to have a correct appreciation of the contributions and value of a man's or a woman's flesh and blood, or face or figure, of what is frequently regarded as the mere animal part of their constitution,—to their moral or spiritual life and strength. And Mrs. Besant has been exceptionally favoured by Nature in this respect. She has a fine figure, the beauty and nobility of which even age has not dared to deeply touch. But for a slight tendency to obesity, her contours might well have been described as classical. Though she is, as she herself says,—three-fourths Irish, her face, however, is unmistakably British. Yet I do not remember to have seen another purely British face like Mrs. Besant's that had absolutely not the least little suggestion of the beef-and-beer-bred-up heredity of John Bull in it. And the most remarkable thing in Mrs. Besant's physical constitution is its extreme sensitiveness to what may be called psychic influences. I have often times seen a weird halo playing about her face as she warmed up to her subject while addressing large and entranced audiences. Her perfect elocution may be,— indeed is,—the fruit of long and labourious training of her voice. Her gestures may be due to her natural histrionic endowments. But this strange halo that encircles her face and head as she speaks, no art or training could produce. It is undoubtedly due to her immense psychic endowments. It shows the almost perfect harmony that exists between her body and her mind, and is a proof of the absolute purity of both. Judged by current standards. Mrs. Besant would not I am afraid, be accepted as a pattern of female beauty. In fact, those who have seen her old photographs, that have preserved her youthful figure, may even recognise a slight suggestion of masculinity in her face. Yet there is something in it which exerts a strange fascination over the observer. I first saw her portrait, over five and twenty years ago, in the *Review* of *Reviews.* And I have not forgotten the impression it made upon my mind. That impression was very much deepened when I first, saw her upon a public platform in Calcutta. And since then, almost every time I have seen her, I have felt that here was a woman of whom it might well be said, in the words of Emerson, that—"the soul is wholly embodied, and the body is wholly ensouled."

"Her pure and eloquent blood,
Spoke in her cheeks, and so distinctly wrought,
That one might almost say her body thought."

MRS. BESANT'S BRAHMACHARYA

Such perfect attunement between body and soul is a proof of the purity of her life. According to Hindu experience it is impossible to acquire a physical constitution like that of Mrs. Besant, without the strictest observance of the disciplines of Brahmacharya. We may not accept her pretensions to what they call adept-hood in Theosophical parlance. We may even question her title to true discipleship. But we cannot disregard occular evidence and refuse to accept her as a true Brahmacharinee. And it shows the wonderful self-mastery of this remarkable woman. A rebel against established faiths and morals at a most critical period of her life, Mrs. Besant has waded through many dirty doctrines, and has even been thrown a good deal into many Bohemian sets, but her body and, one might even add her mind also, have passed through all these, without the least taint of any evil. Indeed, it has sometimes seemed to me, as I read, of her life, among free thinkers and secularists, that she has been built differently from ordinary men and women, and is constitutionally free from the vulgar cravings of our common flesh. But whether it is constitutional or acquired, her self-mastery is undeniable; and it is manifest in the purity of her life and the large psychic powers which that purity has helped to develop.

THE PSYCHIC PLANE AND THE SPIRITUAL PLANE

That Mrs. Besant possesses very large psychic powers, it seems impossible to deny. Those who are anxious to deny these, seem to me to be simply confusing the psychic plane with the true spiritual plane. We now and then come across hysteric women with extraordinary psychic endowments, whose powers of both clairvoyance and even clairaudience are undeniable, yet who occupy a very low spiritual plane, in fact whose spirituality is scarcely higher than that of their pet dog or their Persian puss. And the reason of it is also plain. The psychic plane reaches as far as our Manas — the true rendering of which is not the mind, but the sensorium. Our psychic life is, therefore, very largely, if not entirely, determined and dominated by our nervous system. The keen and quick responsiveness of the nerve centres, is a condition of psychic development. Both clairvoyance and clair-audience imply a supersensitivenees of the optic and the auditory nerves. This supersensitiveness may be attained by a variety of means. It may sometimes result from abnormal conditions, as in neurotic subjects. It may be acquired also under healthy conditions by carefully selected physical and psycho-physical exercises that go by the common name of yogic practices. These practices create certain physical conditions, induce a certain state of the nervous system, which are of very great help to the spiritual life, but that have no necessary relation, as of cause and effect, to that life. High spiritual life does develop large yogic powers, but these powers may, and not infrequently do, exist without any lofty spirituality. Numerous instances of exceptionally large yogic powers in most vile and vicious men and women, are mentioned even in the recognised and authoritative text books on Yoga. Neither ancient Hindu wisdom nor modern Hindu saints and sages make, therefore, any confusion between psychic life and spiritual powers. Right reason, right emotions, right endeavour and right action, these are the true test of the spiritual life. But they may or may not be found in highly developed psychic subjects. And the value of these terms is determined by their direct, constant, and conscious reference to the Universal. Right reason thus, is that which moves and works always in the Universal as the True. Right emotion is, similarly, that which always lives and moves in the Universal as Rasa — He is Rasa: by gaining this rasa, all creatures enjoy themselves,—as we have it in the Upanishads. Right effort is that which is moved by a consciousness of the Universal as Sivam or the Good. And right action is that which is without the least little reference to the agent's own self-regarding desires, but which aims at universal well-being. These are the characteristics of the spiritual life, as we have always known and understood it in India.

THE PHILOSOPHY OF THE SPIRITUAL LIFE

It may, however, be questioned whether Mrs. Besant can be justly credited with any exceptionally high spiritual acquisitions of this type. She has great gifts. Exceptionally pure in body, quick of understanding, strong of will, Mrs. Besant is also endowed with considerable psychic powers, which almost invariably go with large spiritual acquisitions. These powers are however only the inseparable accidents of high spiritual life, but they do not, of themselves, constitute that life nor are an absolute proof of its presence. The real spiritual life is different from the intellectual, the ethical, and even the emotional life, as it admittedly is from our physical life, though it always finds outer expressions in and through all these. The true test of this spiritual life is the conscious identification of the individual with the Universal in every department and activity of his life. It manifests itself in three ways. One is the way of Jnanam or Gnosis. The other is the way of Bhakti or love. And the third is the way of Karma or works. But behind these three-fold ways of the true spiritual life, there is always present, whether explicitly, or implicitly, a special philosophy of life. And that philosophy is fundamentally Monistic. The philosophy that we learn from books or to which our intellectual convictions may attach themselves as the result of our own reasoning or ratiocination, is not always the real philosophy of our life. The former may be a mere matter of speculation. The latter must always be the final result and generalisation of the sum total of our inner experience. Consequently, it is not always necessary that our real philosophy of life should have any vital and organic relation to our ordinary intellectual convictions or our traditional beliefs. The truly spiritual man may, therefore, be a pronounced dualist in his intellectual convictions, but in the depths of his inner consciousness, standing in the light of his beatific experiences, he is, and must be, a pure monist. No one suspects any tinge or taint of monism or pantheism in the ethical teachings of Jesus. But in his innermost consciousness, Jesus was undoubtedly a monist or he could have never said—"I and my Father are One." In his high spiritual life Jesus had fully realised the unity of his individual self with the Universal: and this declaration is only an authoritative assertion of that unity. As in Judaism so also in Islam, there is really no suspicion of what is usually called pantheism. Yet one cannot study the lives of the Mahomedan saints of Persia or Arabia, without being profoundly impressed with their abiding consciousness of the Universal. In fact, a very slight acquaintance with the literature of the true spiritual life all the world over reveals some sort of philosophical monism and idealism the back of it.

THE EVOLUTION OF MRS. BESANT'S PHILOSOPHY

It may not, however, be very easy to discover Mrs. Besant's real philosophy of life. She has professed and preached so many different and even contradictory doctrines, that it is no easy thing to find out either the least common multiple or the greatest common measure of her strange and rich intellectual repertory. Yet there must be some sort of a secret unity or affinity even in these strange collections or they could never have found a place in an individual intellectual life and evolution. Mrs. Besant's changes have been somewhat violent, and one cannot indeed feel sure even now that she has reached the last of these. Nor do they prove any serious mental or moral disqualification. The men or women who change not from youth to age, except in the body, may be considered very steady and respectable, but whether they actually live or simply vegetate may also be very partinently questioned. And whatever else Mrs. Besant has or has not done, there can, I think, be absolutely no question about the fact that she has lived her life and not simply vegetated. She has changed many a time. But changes have no meaning unless they are worked upon something that persists, unchanged, through all these changes. There is something, somewhere, persistent and everpresent,- something that is vainly seeking to find itself through all these changes, even in the most volatile person. That something is at once the least common multiple and the greatest common measure of our changing lives. It is that something which constitutes the most vital element in our real philosophy of life. To understand the value of Mrs. Besant's spiritual life one must seek and discover this permanent and persistent factor of her inner life and character.

Born a. Christian, married to a priest of the established Church in England her first intellectual allegiance was naturally given to the creeds and dogmas of popular Protestant Christianity. Nor was she a half-hearted Christian, either. Mrs. Besant's forceful nature never can engage itself half-heartedly in any persuit, whether intellectual or moral, social or religious. She believed in every Christian doctrine, faithfully followed the religious exercises of the Church, and threw herself with unstinted enthusiasm into the parochial works of her husband's congregation. But all of a sudden, a domestic calamity, the death of her only child, a daughter to whom she was much devoted, scattered her house of sands. She could not reconcile this death, this cruel crushing of a life so tender, so lovely, so full of hope and promise,—"with the presence of a God who is Good, in this world. Mill's problem faced her. Why is there death, disease, sorrow, degradation, vice, sin,—all these multitudinous evils in this world ? How are these reconciled with the beneficence of the responsible Ruler of the Universe ? The only answer that Mill found for this question was that God is either not-good, or He is not-powerful enough to keep down evil. This view of the world-problem destroys either the benevolence or the omnipotence of the Deity. In other words, it banishes God altogether from this world. Mrs. Besant thus found out by bitter personal experience,—or more correctly speaking, she thought that she had discovered,—that there was no God like the God whom she had all her life believed in and prayed to.

Many people, especially in our age, losing the faith of their fathers, gradually drift into some kind of philosophical agnosticism. In fact, this agnosticism is the general trend of the highest generalisations of modern science. The scientist finds himself surrounded by such endless mysteries which baffle all his logic and his thought, that a confession of ignorance is his only natural course. Science, therefore, in the usual sense of the term, is fundamentally agnostic. It refuses to assert that which it does not know and cannot verify. But to some intellects a confession of ignorance is absolutely impossible. These intellects can never say—I do not know. They must assert themselves as much in their assertion of what they profess to know, as in that of what they admit they do not know. Mrs. Besant's intellect is distinctly of this type. Her unbelief became, therefore, more than mere agnosticism, it developed into positive atheism. This intellectual assertiveness has been a prominent feature of her character. It was equally present in her early Christianity, as in her subsequent atheism and secularim. It was a prominent feature in her subsequent Theosophy also. What did not exist to her, could not exist in the universe. What was true to her, must be true universally and for all. In theory, Theosophy has little room, really, for any kind of absolutism. A system or doctrine that proclaims the truth of *all* religions, which believes, like Hinduism, in evolution and adhikariveda—in the religious and the spiritual life, cannot be absolutist in any sense of the term. In practice, however, like many other universalist doctrines, Theosophy is clearly, absolutist. It is, therefore, that we so frequently found at one time, an irritating impatience of other ideas and ideals, other doctrines and diciplines, in Mrs. Besant. In India her condemnation of almost all our modern religious movements, whether of the Brahmo Samaj or of the Arya Samaj or of the Vedantic propaganda of Swami Vivekananda, had at one time been both exceedingly narrow and exceedingly bitter. This narrowness was inconsistent with the true spirit of Theosophy. This bitterness is unknown in those who have attained high spiritual life, at least in India, and among the Hindus. But I do not blame Mrs. Besant for it. These things are constitutional in her. All extraordinarily ardent natures are narrow : and absolute devotion to a particular school or system or sect naturally, breeds bitter antagonism against opposite or rival schools, systems or sects. It is only when these ardent and devoted souls attain superior spiritual elevation, or are called to some large practical work, needing combined and organised efforts of many minds of diverse castes and culture that these limitations drop off their mind and character like the dry leaves of autumn.

MRS. BESANT'S SELF-CENTREDNESS

This absolutism is a common feature of all prophetic temperaments in this world. People with a mission—and Mrs. Besant undoubtedly believes, herself to be one—cannot get rid of it. The one fixed idea that possesses or obssesses the prophetic minds is that they are specially made for the world, and the world is specially made for them or their mission. We see it even in Jesus. It is prominent in Mahomet. It is very common in all the great Jewish prophets. And it is not at all surprising that it should be so marked a feature in Mrs. Besant's character also. For she too, undoubtedly, has this prophetic temperament. Whether one agrees with Mrs. Besant or not, one cannot reasonably deny that she is made of the stuff of which the world's prophets are made. She has the same purity of flesh, the same psychic powers, the same magnetic presence, the same fervour of spirit, the same gift of the tongue, the same powerful imagination, and the same self-confidence and self-consciousness, that are characteristic of the prophets of the world.

And this excessive self-consciousness stands out very prominently of all the multitudinous changes that Mrs. Besant has passed through. Her revolt against Christian Theism was not the fruit of any deep reflection on the meaning and *rationale* of the Christian doctrine. The prevailing unbelief and scepticism of the later eighteenth and the middle-nineteenth century in Europe, was the result of the new criticism which the progress of modern science called into being. Not to mention Mill or Bentham, Tyndell or Huxley, Spencer or Frederick Harrison—to cite a few British names only, even Charles Bradlaugh's so-called atheism was the result of his mental speculations and intellectual temperament. But Mrs. Besant's early atheism was not of this type. She did try, no doubt, to present her ideas in a scientific garb,—and her reading of scientific literature has also been very considerable; but still it can hardly be held that she was driven out of the orthodox Christian fold, by any insuperable intellectual difficulty. These difficulties came afterwards to support and strengthen her revolt, but did not themselves originate it. Her rationalism and secularism was not the fruit of reflection and criticism, but they seemed to have emerged out of a sudden shock caused by the illness and death of her only child. It was not her intellect but her emotions that first raised the standard of revolt. And even these emotions were not of the highest order. The blow that laid her prostrate was really physical, it was due to the annihilation of her sense-relations with her beloved daughter. Death pains us so terribly simply by breaking up our sense-relations and carnal communion with our beloved ones on earth. All grief is, therefore, carnal and absolutely self-regarding. It was a great grief that broke up Mrs. Besant's old faith in God. And it means, in plain English, that because her little girl had the measles and died of it, Mrs. Besant saw no justification for a God to exist, or to pretend to be Good and Omnipotent, in this world. The whole universal order was created for Mrs. Besant and her little family. This is really what this revolt meant. All the science and logic with which she supported her atheistic propaganda came, thus, not first, but subsequently, to justify and strengthen her emotional revolt. It was neither science nor logic that really destroyed Mrs. Besant's earlier religion. It was rather Death that killed her God.

HER LACK OF DISCRIMINATION

And that death could play such hovoc with Mrs. Besant's life was due to two things; first her supersensitive nervous constitution, and second her lack of discrimination, between the soul and the body. This lack of discrimination is almost universal in this world, yet if death does not create such revolutions in our lives, it is because our natures are shallow, and we have not that capacity to feel anything, whether pleasure or pain, so overwhelmingly as some people. Mrs. Besant has this capacity. This extreme sensitiveness is, indeed, a characteristic of all superior psychic constitutions. Had Mrs. Besant been less psychically endowed, or had she any real spiritual life in her, her child's death would not have touched her so deeply. She had professed the Christian faith. She had followed the outer, ethical laws of her Church. Her faith was sincere, but still it was merely traditional and not reasoned. She received it from others, it was not the fruit of her personal experience. Her loyalty to the regulations of her Church was also unflinching. But we do not get real spiritual life from these things. To get that life one must be born again. And the process of this birth is baptism, not as the Churches administer it, but as Christ knew and understood it, and as He exemplified it in His own life. It was only, as He emerged out of the waters of Jordan, after His initiation by John, that Jesus received His recognition as the Son of God:—"This is my Son in whom I am well pleased." In our language, we call it *Gurukaranam* the acceptance of a Guru by the disciple and the acceptance of the disciple by his Guru, as a fit subject to receive the initiatory sacrament. And during this ritual, the spiritual life that is fully developed in the Guru, passes on to the disciple, through what is called *Sakteesanchara* or the transmission of spiritual power. These are things which are, practically, unknown to the practice of the Churches in Christendom, as well as to popular religious rituals in Hinduism, Mrs. Besant never had this true baptism administered to her. She had, therefore, not been born in the spirit. Her *viveka*—or discrimination between the body and the soul,—had not yet been awakened. Her sense of identity between the body and the soul had not yet been destroyed. And all this accounts at once for the destruction of her old faith and the birth of her new scepticism and atheism.

MATERIALISM AND OCCULTISM

In fact, one hardly feels quite sure if Mrs. Besant got rid of her old emphasis on the sense-life and her faith in sense-testimony even in her early years in the Theosophic fold. She has for many years past been a great preacher of occultism. And all occultism is, indeed, occular, that is, really sensuous. All miracles however produced, appeal finally, not to our inner but to our outer senses, for their truth and verification. Occultism need not be dismissed as false. Miracles need not be voted as impossible. All our saints and sages believed in these. They have borne testimony to their truth and possibility. But, all the same, they have set little or no value on these, as factors or the proofs of the spiritual life. On the contrary, higher Hindu thought has always discouraged the tendency to seek these powers to work signs and wonders, regarding them as hindrances to real spiritual progress, when they are deliberately sought. For, after all, though they indicate, in certain cases, the domination of matter by the spirit, and the consequent superiority of thought over matter, and of the soul over the senses, yet these signs and wonders help to bind us to the sensuous and the material plane, and do not really liberate us from their bondage. And as one recognises this lack of discrimination, or *viveka* in Mrs. Besant's first revolt against Christianity, and sees her dependence on the senses made fully manifest in her secularist propaganda, so one cannot completely get rid of the suspicion that it lay hidden even at the back of the impulse that drove her from the gross secularism of the school of Charles Bradlaugh to the subtle occultism of Madame Blavatsky. It was Madame Blavatsky's "ISIS UNVEILED" that led to Mrs. Besant's conversion to Theosophy. And remarkable as that book undoubtedly is, it does not really deal with true spiritual verities as we have always understood them in higher Hindu thought, but only of the secret and unseen forces and powers that dominate man's outer and open material and sense-life and control his evolution. It seeks to explain that many things voted as supernatural, and therefore incredible,—by the votaries of natural science, are not really supernatural. They are as much controlled by natural laws as either heat or light or electricity or any other object or phenomena of the physico-chemical group. It may perhaps be said that Madame Blavatsky naturalised the supernatural, superfined the sensuous, and reduced the grosser material contents of our experience into subtle etherialities : that is all. But all her superfinities and etherialities were still very different from true spirituality. "Isis Unveiled" goes very far, and very high indeed, into the psychic plane only, but not to the real spiritual plane as it is understood in higher Hindu culture.

MRS. BESANT AND MADAME BLAVATSKY

And this is the secret, I think, of the strange hold that the " Isis Unveiled" took of Mrs. Besant's imagination. There was, in the first place, considerable affinity between the inner nature of Madame Blavatsky and that of Mrs. Besant. Both were highly developed psychic subjects. Both were also, profoundly rationalistic and sceptic, though Madame Blavatsky's scepticism was covered by an exuberant supernaturalism. All her atheistic professions notwithstanding, Mrs. Besant could not find complete solace in the realm of the grossly sensuous. Her keen psychic instincts forced upon her, one might say almost against her will, the insufficiency of the merely materialistic explanation of life and its experiences. Her scientific readings told her that what is ordinarily called matter is not self-sufficient. There is force behind the atoms, that shaped and moulded this cosmos out of primordial chaos. And this force, though revealed to the senses through its works and effects, is yet, in itself, absolutely supersensuous. The suggestion of the Unknown, the Unseen, the Immaterial is present in every act and experience of the senses. All these, even the atheist and the secularist could not refuse to admit. What really troubles them is the wide and impassable gulf which popular religion creates between the seen and the unseen, between matter and spirit. In Madame Blavatsky's presentation of the unseen, there was no such gulf. The spirit was only etherialised matter. The Supernatural was not an antethesis of the Natural but only its perfection and fulfilment,—a higher stage of its own natural evolution. There is no absolute contradiction, thus, between the unseen and the seen; they are really one, like two ends of one and the same stick. The difference between them is that one is subtle and superfine, the other is gross and crude. It was thus, it seems to me, that Madame Blavatsky's " Isis Unveiled" bridged the gulf between the natural and the so-called supernatural, that had been troubling Mrs. Besant. This is how she saw a new Light in Madame, and went to her with all the passionate ardour of her nature.

PSYCHOLOGY OF MRS. BESANT'S CONVERSION

Superficial observers characterised Mrs. Besant's sudden conversion from rank atheism and secularism of the Bradlaugh School to the Theosophy of Madame Blavatsky as a wild somersault. But upon careful analysis it will be found, I think, as a most easy and logical process of regular development. It is notorious that both Madame Blavatsky and Colonel Olcott were Buddhists of the Southern School which is distinctly agnostic, if not atheistic. Neither Madame Blavatsky nor Colonel Olcott believed in God. Their intellectual allegiance was paid to what is called Buddhistic Nihilism or the *Bauddha Sunyavada* as it is described in our literature. The universe is uncaused or self-caused and moves around its own axis, by its own force or law, without the action or intervention of any one who is its creator or governor. As the seed grows from the fruit, and the fruit from the seed; so the cosmic process is an endless and uncaused series. And in this series there is, and can be, no real difference between what is popularly called matter and what is called mind. Mind proceeds from matter and matter proceeds again from mind. Spirit is etherialised matter, matter is concretised and sensualised spirit. And man himself is the maker of his own destiny. He thinks, and he is; he wills and he becomes. And when one considers these fundamental concepts of the Theosophical Doctrine of Madame Blavatsky and Colonel Olcott, one feels really no surprise that Mrs. Besant, as soon as she became acquainted with it, embraced it with all her mind, and all her heart and all her strength.

SECULARISM AND THEOSOPHY

Even as a secularist, Mrs. Besant had her high ideals. She had lost faith in the God of the Church in which she was brought up; but she still retained her faith in Man. She believed in the ethical perfectibility of the human race. Her ethics was hedonistic, no doubt;

happiness was to her the goal of life. But still it rested upon her innate faith in the almost endless possibilities of the human life, here on earth. At the back of all the denials of Charles Bradlaugh there was a profound sense of the utter impotence of man. I once heard him exclaim—"we all know, what little man can do;" and he put, it seemed to me, the experience of a life-time into that short sentence, every sound of which seemed to receive a lively response from every atom of his flesh, every drop of his blood, and every tissue of his nerve-cells. I am not sure if Mrs. Besant had in her secularist days, any deep sense of this impotence of man as Charles Bradlaugh had it. The idea finds little support from the general tenour of her inner life and make. On the contrary, in the Theosophical Doctrine of Madame Blavatsky Mrs. Besant found a new support of her inner confidence in the power of man to work out his own happiness or salvation or destiny by whatever name we may call his ultimate end, —himself. Mrs. Besant's revolt against the Christian's God was due to the fact that that God would not or could not make her happy, enable her to fight and conquer death. But neither her atheism nor her secularism could solve that root-problem for her. Denial of God does not banish Death; nor does disbelief in the beyond, —which is the fundamental fact in secularism—disprove the presence of this terrible fact of life. If, therefore, intellectually her atheism and secularism could not bridge the gulf between the seen and unseen, so ethically these could not bridge the gulf between the here and hereafter. In the Theosophical Doctrine, as Madame Blavatsky and Colonel Olcott understood and preached it,—there was some sort of a solution of these difficulties. Theosophy, as Madame Blavatsky and Colonel Olcott understood it, did not posit any God, like that of the Christians or the Mahomedans or even our own Vaishnavas or Saivites of the Siva-Jnana-bodhinee School,—and had, therefore, no open conflict with atheism. Even atheists cannot deny the existence of some ultimate reality, from which the universe is evolving: only they refuse to attribute intelligence or will or love or goodness to it. In other words, the difference between atheists and agnostics on the one side, and theists, whether Hindu, or Christian, or Moslem on the other, consists fundamentally in their respective conception of that ultimate Reality which the former consider impersonal and unconscious, the latter believe to be personal and self-conscious. And the Buddhistic School to which Madame

Blavatsky and Colonel Olcott belonged, held the former position. They did not believe in the Personality of God. But they believed in the unseen. They believed in soul and in the endless possibilities of this soul. The soul's *karma* creates all its material vehicles for itself. The soul again by right culture, can sever this endless chain of karma and attain Nirvana, passing beyond both life and death. Theosophy, thus, without demanding of Mrs. Besant a surrender of her atheism and secularism offered her an easy way out of the difficulties that these had created in her intellectual and moral life. It worked, therefore, only a transfiguration of her old secularism and atheism, but not a true conversion of Mrs. Besant into beliefs totally different from what she previously had.

THE ROLE THAT THEOSOPHY PLAYED

This was, indeed, the special *role* which Theosophy came to play in the moral and intellectual evolution of our time. It found a refuge for those whose capacity for the true spiritual life had been practically destroyed by modern materialism. Even great spiritual teachers had sometimes used these Theosophical methods for the conversion of the faithless. Christ's miracles were admittedly meant for those "of little faith." They could not have believed in his lofty spiritual teachings, if he had not supported these by signs and wonders. The older religions had lost their hold on our generation. Most of them were too other-worldly, laid too much stress on the unseen or the spiritual to have any message for large numbers of those whose minds had been unsettled by modern rationalism. The emancipation of the intellect which modern science, and modern social, economic and political movements combined to work out, deprived the representatives of the older religions of their ancient authority over the laity. The older moorings of the religious life were thus completely destroyed for large numbers of people in every part of the world. It was so in Christendom. It was even so here in India, where the new illumination brought by the British rulers, unsettled people's faiths and created a large body of deistic or sceptic opinion in the country. The Brahmo Samaj and the Arya Samaj did try to offer some sort of a readjustment; but the postulates of both these reformed religious movements warred more or less, against the fundamental ideas of that, secularism and free-thought, which was responsible for this prevailing unbelief. The position of neither was sufficiently logical. Neither Brahmic intuitions nor the Vedic authority of the Arya Samaj touched the root of the problem that troubled large numbers of the modern-educated classes among us. What these people wanted was a "demonstrated" and "demonstrable" religion,—a religion, that could be tested and verified by the same or by similar kinds of evidence upon which the sciences work. Neither the older religions nor these modern reforms could do this. Theosophy offered to do it. It appealed to signs and wonders. It claimed to produce phenomena on the plane of the senses which ordinary sense-experience could not explain. Its missionaries spirited away articles of dress or ornament from people's body, and discovered these in places where no human agency, as we understand it, could have placed them. The first success of Theosophy, in India, was at Mrs. Hume's house at Simla. This was followed by others. The transmission of missives through the ceiling, the discovery of Kuthoomilal's pugree somewhere, thought-reading, hypnotism, clairvoyance, clairaudience, materialisation of immaterial thought, and the spiriting away into empty space of gross and tangible and solid materialities,—all these helped to recreate the faith of good many people in the unseen and the supersensuous, who had lost it altogether. And these signs and wonders were accompanied by interpretations of both mind and matter, which in no way warred against the prevailing materialistic theory of the universe. Theosophy did not ask people to believe in a God or to pray to Him. It did not ask them to believe in a spiritual world which was not only different from, but was, in many respects, contrary to the visible world of matter and sense. It simply worked or pretended to work miracles; and declared that these were not supernatural but only the application of hidden or lost knowledge of natural laws, more subtle and, therefore, more powerful than those which modern science called such. It did not banish death by any lofty spiritual philosophy such as we find, for instance, in the Bhagavat-Geeta,—but simply proved the possibility of indefinitely postponing death by certain disciplines, and pointed out to the *Mahatmas* as men who had attained this indefinite, if not everlasting, life, through these means. Thus, Theosophy found what may be called a half-way-house between infidelity and faith, for large numbers of people whom no purely spiritual appeal could influence at that time.

THEOSOPHIC MORALS AND UNIVERSALISM

But though all may not accept the spiritual pretensions of Theosophy, as preached by Madame Blavatsky and Colonel Olcott, no one can reasonably refuse to admit its ethical and humanitarian claims. In fact, it was these latter that drew good many people into the Theosophical Society, especially when it first started work in this country, who had no sympathy with the theology of its founders. Even occultism has a supreme ethical reference. The training of the will is an essential element of the cultivation of occult powers. The development of a healthy sensitiveness of the nerve-centres is another requirement of it. And all these demand the strictest discipline of our animal instincts and appetites. Libertinism and occultism can never go together. Strict regimen, rigid abstinence, regular habits, observance of the rules of holiness, in the old-world sense of *taboo,*— all these are counted as Theosophic disciplines; and all these make for a pure and self-restrained life. In spite of their undeniable physical reference, the ethical value of these disciplines cannot be reasonably questioned. Many people whom modern secularism and "free-thought" had gradually driven to gross sensualities and intemperance, turned altogether a new leaf in their life under the influence of Theosophy. It visibly broadened their outlook upon humanity also. It proclaimed a Universal Brotherhood, based not upon a common denial of all faith, but upon an acceptance of every faith and every religion as fundamentally true. And this universalism, whatever its philosophic basis or value, was distinctly broader, and in some sense, even truer than the credal universalism of either Christianity or Islam. No man had to deny anything really, to join the Theosophic Brotherhood. The Hindu, the Buddhist, the Christian, the Mahomedan, the Zoroastrian, the Theist and the Atheist,— all could join it, without giving up their own faiths and beliefs or renouncing their allegiance to their respective social or religious communion or denomination. No other organisation or association except those of a professedly secular character that had for their object the realisation of some definite material or social end,—had before offered such latitude to its members in the matter of their religious beliefs or their social life. The conflict of religions had for ages jarred upon the sensibilities of all refined people. Theosophy offered to settle this conflict, not by denying the claims of any religion in favour of any others, but by declaring that in truth and reality, all religions are one and equally true. In every religion there are two sides: one its outer, popular, exoteric side; the other its inner, refined, esoteric side. All conflicts appear on the exoteric side of the different religions. They are due to gross misunderstanding of the real meaning and purpose even of these outer dogmas, doctrines, rituals, sacraments, disciplines and worships. But on the esoteric side, there is really, no conflict. Esoteric Buddhism is the same, substantially, as Esoteric Christianity. The meaning and purpose of the Grecian Mysteries are similar to, if not the same as those of the Hindu Tantras. The Secret Doctrine of the Moslem Sufis is the same as that of the Hindu Vendantin. And the proclamation of this unity between the different religious systems of the world, based upon the unity of the Secret Doctrine, taught and demonstrated by a body of adepts or Mahatmas, who form a secret brotherhood among themselves,—appealed to many people who had been groping after some sort of a universal religion or church which would cancel all religious conflicts, and build up a universal brotherhood among the races of the world. These are the secrets of the hold that Theosophy took of many people both here and in Europe and America in the last quarter of the last century. All these explain also the strange spell that it cast over so rebellious a spirit as Mrs. Besant.

Mrs. BESANT'S CONTRIBUTIONS TO THEOSOPHY

Mrs. Besant's conversion became, in fact, the salvation of the Theosophical Society. She not only lent a new inspiration to it by her wonderful eloquence, but added distinctly new elements to the whole thought-structure of the movement. Madame Blavatsky had emphasised the occult teachings of Theosophy. Colonel Olcott had emphasised its ethical and humanitarian side. The revelations of the Columbs considerably shook public confidence in the truth and honesty of Madame Blavatsky, and threw considerable discredit upon occultism itself. For a time the whole movement was under a cloud. It is, indeed, very doubtful if the Theosophical Society could have lived all that evil-repute down, if Mrs. Besant had not come to the rescue. Madame Blavatsky and Colonel Olcott had both of them dropped down upon us almost from the clouds. Little was known of their antecedents. But Mrs. Besant's case was different. For years before she joined the Theosophical Society, she had been a well known person in England. Her life was as an open book to all the world. Her veracity was above suspicion. Her intellectual integrity was absolutely unquestioned. Whatever else this remarkable woman could or could not do, of one thing everybody who knew her either personally or by repute, felt absolutely sure, and it was that she could never be false to her own self. The conversion of Mrs. Besant, helped, therefore, to somewhat recreate the faith of good many people not perhaps in the integrity of Madame Blavatsky, but, at any rate, in the truth, at least, of occultism. Mrs. Besant. however, started to work almost from the very commencement of her career as an apostle of Theosophy, to remove the old emphasis on occultism, and to import an element of attractive metaphysical speculations and spiritual idealism into the Theosophic movement. Her metaphysics may or may not be sound. Her spirituality may or may not be deep or high. But that she has given a colour of both to Theosophical teachings none can deny. And in so doing she, practically, freed these from the taint of that agnosticism with which both Madame Blavatsky and Colonel Olcott had been notoriously identified and placed her Theosophy in a close and vital relation with the highest thoughts and speculations of the Hindus. In India, at least, the Theosophical movement, under Mrs. Besant's leadership, became almost openly allied to, if not absolutely identified with, the Hindu Revival of the closing decades of the last century. And this is, I think, the real secret of the wonderful hold that she soon took of the thoughts and aspirations of a good many of our English educated people.

MRS. BESANT'S CONTRIBUTIONS TO THE HINDU REVIVAL

In one sense, the Theosophical Society was, from the day it came to India, more or less allied to this Hindu Revival Movement. The Brahmo Samaj was, in fact, the first and earliest expression of the revived consciousness of Hinduism, quickened by its first impact with Christian propagandist and European rationalism. It stemmed the course of both among the English educated classes, offering them a religion that was at once rational in its philosophy and national in its spirit and form. Gradually, however, the Brahmo Samaj under Keshub Chunder Sen became possessed with an ideal of abstract cosmopolitanism that weakened the old nationalist note of the movement, and gradually became more allied, both in spirit and form, to Christian thought and history than to those of Hinduism. The Hindu Revival Movement which practically synchronised with the advent of the Theosophical Society in India was, in fact, a protest against cosmopolitanism of the Brahmo Samaj. Theosophy lent considerable strength to this revival, by its new message of what it called "Ancient Wisdom." This ancient wisdom, as Colonel Olcott and Madame Blavatsky understood it, was not entirely Indian. It was the wisdom of all the ancients, Assyrians, Babylonians, Egyptians, Hindus, all alike. It was the secret doctrine of all the ancient cults. But still among us in India, this appeal had the direct effect of creating a new interest in our modern-educated classes, in the old scriptures of the country. The study of the old Upanishads was revived. And, I think, after Raja Ram Mohun Roy, it was the Theosophists of India, who first commenced to publish English translations of the more canonical of these ancient scriptures. Notwithstanding all this, however, there was as yet no direct reference in the teachings of the Theosophical Society, to the popular religion of our people. The ancient Hindu wisdom that Colonel Olcott and Madame Blavatsky preached recreated people's faith in the old religion of their country, yet, offered but little explanation or justification of our current ceremonialism, and absolutely no open apology for our social economy.

THEOSOPHY AND HINDU REVIVAL

All this was left to beldone by Mrs. Besant, Colonel Olcott and Madame Blavatsky had only helped the movement of Hindu Revival from the outside. They inspired large numbers of our English-educated classes with a profound reverence for the past spiritual acquisitions of their race, and thereby stemmed simultaneously the tide of both Christian and Brahmo propagandism among us. Their work was, thus, in a way more or less negative. They offered no apology for current religion, but simply tried to justify popular supernaturalism. They claimed some element of truth and reality for what may be called the magic and sorcery, the *mantra,* and the *tantra,* of lower Hinduism, but did not touch the vital problems of either caste or idolatry. Mrs. Besant commenced to tackle these difficult problems. Colonel Olcott occasionally talked of the Buddha. Both he and Madame Blavatsky always spoke with bated breath of the mysterious Mahatmas from whom they claimed to derive both their instruction and their inspiration. But, neither the Buddha nor these Mahatmas had any reference either to our religious traditions or to our religious life. It was Mrs. Besant who first, among the leaders of the Theosophical Society, commenced to preach the wisdom of Sree Krishna and the Bhagavat-Geeta. The old disciplines of the Theosophical Society were mostly psycho-physical and ethical. Mrs. Besant was the first to import into these what may be called a spiritual element. She did not believe,—not in her earlier years in the Theosophical Society, at any rate, —in what is called the Personality of God. In this she followed in the steps of both Colonel Olcott and Madame Blavatsky. The Hindu Vedantin also, of the Sankara School in any case, does not posit any personality in the Absolute. But even Sankara accepted the personality of *Isvara,* the first and highest emanation from the Absolute or the Brahman in the Mayic series. Popular Hindu thought is very largely Vedantic in this respect. It is only Vaishnava Vedanta which accepts the Personality of the Supreme. I doubt it very much if Mrs. Besant has advanced to this highest Vaishnavic standpoint; but that she went as far as the Isvara of the Sankara Vedanta cannot be denied. In this, her philosophy was a distinct advance upon the older philosophy, at least of the founders, of the Theosophical Society. It was a clear advance from Buddhistic rationalism and ethicism, to the imaginative Hinduism of the Puranas. Indeed, Mrs. Besant went still further. She even more or less openly allied herself to the so-called idolatry of popular Hinduism. She did not condemn this idolatry, not even by implication, as might well be said of Madame Blavatsky and Colonel Olcott. The very fact that these Theosophical teachers emphasised the teachings of the Upanishads that have no suspicion of any image-worship, as embodying highest Hindu wisdom, and ignored the later phases of Puranic Hinduism, was a silent but significant condemnation of these. Mrs. Besant, however, stood up as a defender of these. Her explanation of the value of this so-called idolatry was not orthodox. It was, really, secular and materialistic. Our fathers would rise up in anger against Mrs. Besant's suggestion that the merit of these images lay in the mesmeric potency communicated to them by the potter—for it is the potters who make these—and then by the priest. They did not believe in the identity of these images with their dieties; but they believed that during worship the divine spirits do come and possess those symbols and, through them, accept the homage of their devotees. But to a generation steeped in modern scepticism, yet anxious to hold on to the current ceremonials of their people, Mrs. Besant's was the only kind of exegis that could possibly have any value. Whatever their real spiritual or rational value, Mrs. Besant's exegetics therefore did exercise considerable influence over many people who were already losing their faith in the truth of popular Hindu ceremonialism; and who yet, for domestic and social reasons, and possibly also from considerations of the religious emotions, did not quite like the idea of giving up these so-called idolatrous institutions altogether. As in the matter of this so-called idolatry, so in that of our institution of caste also, Mrs. Besant following the Bhagavad-Geeta, sought at one time to somewhat justify and rationalise it. The earlier Hindu reformers, from Keshub Chunder Sen downwards, had all absolutely condemned this institution, and had appealed to their following to openly break through it. Mrs. Besant did not do this. On the contrary, without actually supporting the existing rigidites of caste-exclusiveness, she offered an apology for the original social economy of the Hindus by basing the caste divisions upon *guna* or character and *karma* or occupations; as Sree Krishna had himself done in the

Bhagavad-Geeta. And owing to all this, the Theosophical movement, under Mrs. Besant's leadership, became in the earlier years of her mission, more intimately allied to the movement of Hindu Revival than it had been under Colonel Olcott or Madame Blavatsky. Naturally, therefore, Mrs. Besant has, all these years, exercised an influence over large numbers of our English-educated countrymen including some of the very best and most scholarly of the present generation of Hindus, that has been unapproached and unapproachable by any other person.

Mrs. BESANT'S YOUTHFUL SECULARISM

If Mrs. Besant considerably influenced a large section of English-educated Hindus, by her interpretations of current ideas and institutions of Hinduism, this Hinduism also influenced her thought and life, more profoundly than these had ever been influenced before by any of her previous speculations and activities. The spirit of Hinduism seemed to harmonise with the fundamental philosophy of life that silently, and even unconsciously to herself, had shaped and guided her, ever since she had openly broken away from the faiths and traditions of the English Church. The protest of nineteenth century Rationalism against current Christian dogmas and disciplines was really the protest of individual reason and conscience against the authority of the Scripture and the Church. It was the revolt of the individual against all outside authority. It was really, a fight for personal freedom, which, having largely established itself, through the transformations worked by the French Revolution, in the concepts and constitutions of the State-authority in Europe, now sought to realise itself in the more intimate relations of the domestic, the social, and the religious life. Freedom of citizenship in political life, could not possibly accomodate itself to subjection in the moral or the religious life. Indeed, the protest of the French Revolution was against all outside authority. Its message was the message of complete personal freedom in every department of life. It proclaimed the creation of a New Earth and a New Heaven, wherein all shall be free to think, believe, act, and live, according to their own reason and conscience, after their own mind, without any lot or hindrance from others. Mrs. Besant's revolt against the Church of England was inspired by this demand of the individual to think and act according to his or her own reason and conscience. She denied God, because the God-idea of which she knew in her own country and culture, could not reconcile itself with her reason. She wanted rational proof, and would accept nothing on the authority of the Scriptures or the Church. Modern Science has exploded the theory of the verbal infallibility of the Bible. There are numerous and undeniable errors and mis-statements of positive scientific truths and geographical and historical facts in the Bible. Tom Paine and others had thoroughly exposed these. The destruction of scriptural authority, inevitably dethroned the God who had been set up on it. Many people losing their faith in objective Scriptural authority, had found some foundations for their faith, in subjective intuitions. This theory of Intuition, however, was still in a more or less amorphous condition. It required as much of "faith" to accept the validity of this "Intuition" as was required for the acceptance of the authority of the Scripture. None could claim universality. Neither could offer "positive" evidence, such as the scientific culture of the age demanded. Darwinian Evolution had killed the God of Christian tradition, but had not, as yet, by its own intrinsic logical necessity, discovered the True God of Reason. The sciences had not as yet found their own necessary limitations. The reality of what was described as Matter as well as of what they called Force, had not as yet been discovered. Everything was in a nebulous and unsettled and amorphous state. The only thing that the generation in which Mrs. Besant was born, had fully seized was the Dogma of Individual Liberty. The Supremacy of the Individual Reason and Conscience was the one thing of positive and permanent value which they had fully understood. And as this reason went very little beyond the sensuous plane, all theories were subjected to the test of the senses and inductions and deductions from sense-testimony. This inevitably led to a secularistic philosophy of life and society. This was the inner meaning of Mrs. Besant's youthful secularism. It was really not a gospel of materialism, but only of personal freedom.

There was, however, no room for this personal freedom in Christian tradition and Church authority. This freedom was not recognised by any Theology or Church or Sect with which Mrs. Besant had any acquaintance. There was no freedom in man's religion. Religion was the device of priests and princes to keep the masses in perpetual subjection to their authority. In the name of freedom, therefore, Mrs. Besant declared war against all known religions and theologies.

THE NOTE OF FREEDOM OF THE THEOSOPHIC GOSPEL

In Theosophy she found, for the first time in her life, an organisation which could almost be called religious, that did not demand subscription to any creed or doctrine or dogma, from its members. It declared to them,—"Believe only that which you can see and verify for yourselves." If you have your own convictions, keep them, cherish them, faithfully follow them; only respect the similar beliefs of other peoples in their own faiths. If you are under any discipline, you need not break away from it; only try to understand and realise it that as all roads lead to Rome, so all disciplines, faithfully followed, lead to final Illumination; and realising this, do not quarrel with other disciplines, which may be followed by others with as much sincerity and devotion with which you follow your own way. These elementary ideas and ideals of Theosophy, must have supplied the psychological back-ground of Mrs. Besant's first leanings towards Theosophy.

But Theosophy, as preached by Colonel Olcott and Madame Blavatsky, while appealing to people in the name of religious toleration and human fellowship and universal brotherhood, also declared that all the great world-religions, like Buddhism, Christianity, or Islam, had a dual aspect: one their outer or exoteric aspect, in which they were concerned with external disciplines and rituals, meant for the ignorant and the uninitiated; and the other their inner or esoteric aspect, in which they revealed their real and eternal and fully verified and absolutely verifiable truths, to which only the highest and the most disciplined and refined and spiritual people had full access. The differences and conflicts which men observed between the great world-religions were found only in their outer or exoteric aspects, which dealt with signs and symbols and outer dogmas and disciplines, suited to the different temperaments and social and natural environments of men. But when through these different and diverse dogmas, and symbols, and disciplines and training the devotee reached the higher stages of spiritual evolution, and developed their inner vision, with that illumination they realised the fundamental unity of all religions. Every individual who attained this high spiritual state and illumination saw in the light of his own direct and immediate inner spiritual experience, the fundamental unity of all religions.

And Theosophy declared that that was nothing supernatural, nothing really irrational in this. All religions were one in essence, though diverse in forms. All men have not the same form or feature; yet they are all united in their common manhood or humanity, one in essence but different in form,—one in *ousia,* different in *hypostatis,* to speak in the terms of the Trinitiranian Dogma, — this is the real character of the unity of the human race, which we all fully accept. And the same is the character of the unity of all religions,—one in essence, though different in appearance,—Theosophy proclaimed. This essential unity of all religions was, it further said, quite a demonstrable fact. But all scientific demonstrations required a preliminary training of the senses, and the intellect and a perfection of the instruments of scientific experiment. Without these preliminary sense and mind training and the perfection of the instruments, no scientific truth or theory could be proved to any man. Similarly, religious or spiritual truths for their verification depended upon certain preliminary physical, psycho-physical, intellectual, and spiritual training and qualifications. Within these limits, the highest truths of the religious and the spiritual life are capable of full rational proof and scientific demonstration, as any fact or theory of the physical group of the sciences. "Come to us, accept the disciplines which we suggest, follow the rules of life we lay down, and you will gradually see for yourself what we have seen, verify in your own direct experience the truth of our doctrines and disciplines. We ask you to believe nothing without seeing, to accept nothing on our authority, to deny nothing that you at present believe to be true, to do nothing which does not commend itself to your own reason or your conscience. All that we want is that you should follow the practical training of your body and your mind, a training which will not run counter to your cherished faiths or beliefs, nor in any way outrage your existing religious or social associations or repudiate your social or religious obligations,—and if you follow these innocent and unobjectionable rules of outer and inner life, you will verify yourself the truths of the highest verities of the religious and the spiritual life, which are only another name for what we call "Theosophy."

And, it seems to me, that it was this great Note of Freedom of the gospel of the Theosophical Society, which mainly drew Mrs. Besant to it. This Freedom was the supreme passion of her life. She had broken away from the Church of England, because it sought to restrict the Freedom of her reason and her conscience. She had joined the Socularist propaganda of Mr. Charles Bradlaugh because here she found an organisation which stood up for the supremacy of human reason and the inviolability of the human personality, in every relation of life. She had laboured and suffered through the earlier part of her vigorous womanhood to help men and women to this perfect freedom of thought and speech and action. She had denied the God of Churches and the Scriptures because it was superimposed upon man's minds and lives from the outside and thus hampered their free thinking and free living. She had repudiated the authority of the Church because it sought to reduce living human beings into machines denying both freedom of thought and speech and action to them. And when we view Mrs. Besant's conversion to Theosophy in the light of this supreme passion of her life, we shall see nothing really revolutionary in it. She simply glided, almost imperceptibly to herself, on the wings of this spirit of freedom, from the grosser freedom of the Secularistic Movement to the finer and more scientific freedom of Theosophy.

FROM ATHEISM TO AGNOSTICISM

Indeed, the freedom which the Secularist Movement proclaimed was only half-a-freedom, and not the full measure of it. Secularism was, on the religious and spiritual side, a mere movement of negation. Its loudest note was the note of Denial. No God : No Soul : No life after death : No nothing beyond what was cognised by the outer senses of man; this was the basal teaching of this Secularism. The only positive note of this secularism was that of our sense-life and sense realities. And though it, at first, declared the great institutions of man's religious and spiritual life as the creations of wily and selfish princes and priests, this explanation was too purile to long satisfy the intellectual questionings of the atheists and the sceptics themselves. Modern science demanded a rational explanation of human experience. The earlier explanations of the phenomena of religion were soon found out to be inadequate and irrational. These did not explain all the facts of man's religious life and experience. And scientific reason refused to accept any explanation that failed to explain *all* the facts concerning any phenomena. Secularism failed to explain all the facts of man's religious and spiritual life.

In seeking to find this explanation, Herbert Spencer had arrived at his theory of the unknown and unknowable. He did not deny the truth of the unseen; only declared the inability of the human mind, as it is constituted, to find out what really this unknown is; and therefore the only attribute of this unknown was that it was unknowable. This Spencerian Agnosticism was a great advance upon the atheistic assertions of the earlier secularistic thought of Europe. Numerous people who had hitherto been declared atheists, now commenced to realise the unreasonableness of their position, and cook up the more modest attitude of this Spencerian agnosticism.

Herbert Spencer did another service of supreme value to modern religious thought, by declaring that there was a "Soul of Truth in things erroneous." This great revelation, for so it may well be called, killed the spirit of absolutism as much in current and popular religions as in the prevailing atheism and secularism of the times. It drew the attention of both to the necessary limitations of their respective ideas and beliefs. Scientific proof demanded not merely that an induction should be found wrong, but it must also show *how* that wrong induction could have ever been made. All truth is a matter of experience. And all real experience are true, and the experience itself is its highest and final proof. In presenting these experiences to our own mind, we however, always or almost always, mix them up with our previous experiences, and import into what we directly experience things that stand outside them. Though our experience is a matter of immediate and direct cognition when we relate these experiences to our own mind, we always mix numerous inferences with them. And all our errors and falsehoods are due to these inferences and not really the result of our immediate cognition or experience. This is the basis of the Spencerian dictum that in things erroneous there is a soul of truth.

And it seems to me that the universalism of the Theosophical Society was based, very largely, if not entirely, upon this Spencerian doctrine or dictum. There might be gross errors in man's present religious faiths and the past religious traditions of the race. But these errors too have in them the soul of truth. Errors could never dominate the human race so completely and so powerfully for endless cycles and ages unless they had some soul of truth in them, some basis in their direct experience. And this presumption seemed to have very largely paved the way for the advent of the Theosophical Society in our midst.

All these, namely, the spirit of freedom and toleration, and the recognition of the demands of scientific demonstration for the establishment of religious and spiritual truths, and this declaration of the presence of the Soul of Truth in all religions, however much their outer forms and formularies may seem to be erroneous to us,—all these had a very close affinity with the mental constitution and experiences of Mrs. Besant. But for these deep affinities between the fundamental position of Theosophy and that of this great seeker after truth and freedom, not even the extraordinary magnetism of Madame of Blavatsky's powerful personality could have made a Theosophist of Mrs. Besant.

Whatever superficial students of Mrs. Besant's life and character may say, there is, therefore, really no vital inconsistency in the conversion of the Secularist colleague of Charles Braudlaugh into an honest and ardent disciple of the Theosophist leader Madame Blavatsky. It was really not a case of intellectual somersault, as her enemies say, but only of natural, and indeed, inevitable and logical evolution.

THEOSOPHY AND BUDDHISM

The Theosophical Movement had, from the very beginning, been closely related to certain aspects of ancient Hindu thought. The founders of the Theosophical Society, Col. Olcott and Madame Blavatsky, both professed the Buddhist faith. The reason of it seems to have been the dominant note of agnosticism of some of the Buddhist schools, which had, therefore, very intimate affinity with European rationalism of the last century. The ethical and humanitarian aspects of Buddhistic teachings also may have had a strong fascination for the founders of the Theosophical Society. Buddhistic ethics differs from current Christian ethics in their vital reference to psychology and psychophysics. Christian ethics is mainly instructive while, Buddhistic ethics is constructive. Christianity commands men and women to be good, and leaves, practically, the carrying out of its commandments, to individual effort, particularly to the effort of the individual will. Sin and immorality are regarded by Christian thought fundamentally as a disease of the human will, which is *free* to choose the better way, but does not do so. This freedom of the will is one of the most powerful obsessions of the ethical consciousness of Christendom. It practically looks upon the human will, as a thing apart, which is not organically bound up with the physiological and intellectual structures of the individual. Buddhistic ethics do not assume this isolated freedom of the human will. Buddhistic Ethics are a department of Buddhistic Psychology. In fact, this psychological view of what is called the Ethical Imperative in Christian thought, has been a very marked feature of the entire system of Hindu ethics also. This is why both Hindu and Buddhist ethics have always had a very intimate physiological and psychological reference. It is out of the recognition of this organic connection between physiology, psychology, and ethics, that all our ancient and mediaeval psycho-physical disciplines gradually evolved. This psycho-physical view of the moral life, largely removes the obsession of the idea of the almost absolute freedom of the individual will, which dominates Christian ethics, and thereby brings our will, and with it all our ethical judgments and activities, under the universal dominion of the Law of Causation. This law of Causation, as applied to the ethical life, is called the Law of Karma in both Hindu and Buddhistic thought. This doctrine of Karma is one of the principal planes of Theosophy. This Law of Karma supplied not only a rational hypothesis for our moral life and character, but while repudiating the empirical philosophy of human freedom of popular Christian thought, it made the individual the complete master of his or her destiny. In the lower planes, man is a blind instrument of his Karma. But when, through submission to long and laborious courses of physical, ethical, psychical, and spiritual disciplines, he attains the higher planes of life, the same man becomes a conscious master of his Karma, and through the regulation of his own *karmas,* he may ultimately free himself from the bondage of Karma, and attain final and complete liberation. These views are common to both Hinduism and Buddhism; with this difference that while the Hindu Law of Karma places at the source and top of the Karmic wheel, Iswara or the Lord as the *Karmadhipa* or the Director and Lord of Karma, the Buddhistic schools, with which the founders of the Theosophical Society were associated, recognised no one, except the individual, as the controller and director of his own Karma.

BUDDHISTIC AGNOSTICISM AND INDIVIDUALISM

It will, thus, be seen that as the Buddhistic metaphysics was predominantly Agnostic, so Buddhistic ethics was absolutely Individualistic. In both these aspects, Buddhism bore a very close resemblance to the dominant European thought of the last century. But Buddhistic Individualism was more rational than European Individualism. And, unlike the latter, the Buddhistic theory of the individual, as bound up in the lower stage of the individual evolution with the universal chain of Karma, and identified in the highest stage, with this universal Law, losing in the consciousness of this Law, as part of his own being, all conceits of isolated individuality, —carried with it the message of a Universalism as an organic element of this individualistic philosophy itself, which was unknown to and unappreciated by the Individualistic Rationalism of the Nineteenth Century.

The message of Buddhism, like that of the French illumination of the xviii century, was Equality, Liberty, and Fraternity. But the gospel of Buddhistic Equality did not deny or ignore the actual inequalities of creation, but only declared these as mere incidents of the evolutionary process through which all creation eternally passes; and, as such that these did not repudiate the fundamental unity of the cosmic process or its ultimate aim or end. All can, by working out their Karma, attain final liberation,—themselves become the Buddha. In this all are equal. Buddhistic Liberty also was based upon this final idea of Liberation. This Liberation could not be attained except through submission to long and laborious courses of discipline, which implied subjection. Through subjection to Freedom: this was the message of Buddhism. And, as in its conception of both Equality and Liberty, Buddhism never lost consciousness of the unity of cosmic life and evolution or of the universality of the aim towards which this evolution eternally moves, so the Buddhistic doctrine of Fraternity or *Maitree* also followed as a matter of logical necessity from this doctrines of Equality and Liberty, and was not arbitrarily and mechanically added to these, as we find in the case of the French gospel. Buddhistic metaphysics, and ethics, all therefore offered to supplement and complete, to a very large extent, the half-truths of modern European Rationalism and Individualism. This is why, it seems to me, that Col. Olcott and Madame Blavatsky, who may be said to have fully summed up in their life and thought, the highest elements of this Rationalism and Individualism, accepted Buddhism as their personal faith. And all these must have very powerfully appealed also to Mrs. Besant's inner spirit of rationalism when she first came in contact with Theoso-phical teachings and specially with the powerful personalities of the founders of the Theosophical Society.

BUDDHISTIC AGNOSTICISM AND VEDANTIC GNOSTICISM

I cannot say if Mrs. Besant ever accepted Colonel Olcott's and Madame Blavatsky's Buddhism as her own personal faith. But even if she did, her subsequent evolution from Buddhism to Hinduism cannot be said to have been either unnatural or revolutionary. There is a close affinity between the teachings of the older Upanishads and those of Buddhism. Indeed, the fundamental intellectual and ethical position of Buddhism is the same, practically, as that of these Upanishads. Sankara's interpretations of the Upanishadic doctrine have long been characterised by his critics as "Veiled Buddhistic Nihilism." The Nirguna Brahman of Sankara in some of its aspects, come very close to the Absolute of modern agnostic schools,— the Unknown and Unknowable of Herbert Spencer. Mrs. Besant's earliest acquaintance with Hindu thought was formed through her study of the Upanishads. And the emphasis of all her earlier Theosophical preachings in this country was unmistakably on this Sankara-Vedantic theory of the Nirguna Brahman. At that time she had advanced from her previous rationalistic and atheistic position of the complete denial of God and the soul, to believe in an unknown and unknowable Absolute. She still held to her older denial of a personal God as presented by Christian dogma. All the religious systems known to her at that time, were built upon this dogma of the Divine Personality. In the Upanishads she found for the first time, a system of theology which boldly proclaimed, what may be called, the "impersonality of the Absolute." Here too she found a philosophy of the Absolute, which while fully accepting the fundamental position of Herbert Spencer, namely that the Absolute was unknown,—did not make the unwarranted assertion that It was unknowable also. The Upanishads gave the only rational interpretation that could possibly be given, to this Spencerian doctrine of the Unknown. They said that the Absolute is unknown only in the sense that It cannot be made an *object* of our knowing. In all act of knowing, the subject, conditions its object. But the Absolute cannot be conditioned in any way. Consequently, the Absolute cannot be *known,* as we know our objects. So far the Spencerian dogma is true. But do we know ourselves or not?— know ourselves, that is, as subject or knower, and not as object or known ? If we do, then the Absolute also can be known, similarly, as the *Subject* but not as the object. Thus the Upanishads declared, that the Absolute though Unknown as object, is, however, known as Subject or Self. In our own Self, through our own Self, can the Brahman or the Absolute, be known. In this, the Upanishads while accepting the fundamental truth of modern agnosticism, completely transcended it. The Upanishadic doctrine of the Absolute did not deny but only supplemented and fulfilled the Spencerian dogma of the Unknown and the Unknowable. And as this Spencerian agnosticism was, practically, the last word of modern European Rationalism, the transition from this Rationalism, as happened in the case of Mrs. Besant, to the religion of the Upanishads was neither revolutionary nor irrational. This has been the history of the inner intellectual and religious evolution of many, indeed, of our own English-educated countrymen, who too like Mrs. Besant, found in the Theosophy of these ancient Indian scriptures, a correction and completion of their Rationalism; and who too, like her, discovered in the teachings of these Upanishads, a rational foundation for their faith in the Unseen Cause of all things.

Indeed, it is hardly possible for any thoughtful student of the human mind, to deny the fundamental position of the Upanishads, which posit the Absolute as "That from which all objects have come to being, having come to being, by which all things continue to be, towards which all objects move or through processes of cosmic evolution, and in which all objects find their ultimate end." Not even the rankest atheist or materialist can refuse to accept this proposition; for he too believes in the Law of Causation. Indeed, the first thing that the modern mind revolts against in current religions, is their conception of a Creator, who produced this universe "out of nothing." "Exnihilo, nihil fit," out of nothing, nothing alone can come. The Upanishads declared that this Cosmos has not been brought out of nothing. It has been *evolved* out of that which is called Brahman. This Brahman is both the efficient and the material cause of the universe. This universe is an effect, a *Karyya,* and in every effect or *Karyya* there is, in reality, a transformation of its own cause, or *Karanum.* Brahman is the cause of this universe. This universe is therefore a transformation of the Brahman. The cause exists in its own effect. Brahman therefore, exists in this universe. And every effect moves towards its own cause seeks to realise that, which originated it. The cosmic process moves therefore towards Brahman. This idea of causation is the direct and most valuable contribution of the modern principle or law of evolution, to modern religious speculations. This idea is found completely revealed in the Upanishadic doctrine of the Absolute or Brahman. Here the Absolute is expressed in the terms of what the mathematicians call, x and y. It is an unknown quantity. It is only known as Cause revealed in its own Effect. It says nothing as to what this Cause is in-itself. It attributes nothing to the Absolute, to which anybody can take reasonable exception. And as in an Algebraic Equation, the student has to find out the value of the unknown quantity with which it deals; so even here, in the theology of those Upanishads also, each individual disciple is asked to discover, for himself, the actual value of this Brahman, the existence of which cannot be denied, but the nature of which apart from the fact that it is the Cause of this universe, is unknown. Here there is a far more rational and logical presentation of the Spencerian doctrine or dogma, than is found, I think, even in Spencer himself. And this is why a European rationalist, steeped in the spirit of modern scepticism and agnosticism, naturally finds, through the necessity of his or her own scepticism and agnosticism itself, a satisfactory rational interpretation of his or her own inner ideas and beliefs in our ancient Upanishads. In accepting the theosophy of the Upanishads, Mrs. Besant, therefore, did no violence to her previous convictions, but simply grew into their own latent logical conclusions.

Indeed, the first conclusions of the mind that will apply itself to the solution of the problem of Ultimate Reality, unhampered by any outside or super-imposed faiths, and unaided except by its own logic and the testimony of its own immediate experiences or cognitions, are, and must inevitably be purely materialistic. The Upanishads themselves admit it, as wo find in the Bhrigu-Baruni episode of the Taittiriya Upanishad. The first conclusion of Bhrigu was that the Brahman is Annam. This Annam is the material basis of existence. The Anna-theory of the Absolute means, really, that from primeval matter have all things come into being, by this matter they continue to be, and finally into matter they are resolved. And this is the conclusion of the physio-chemical group of the sciences. But these sciences explain only a part, and, indeed, a very small part really, of our experience. Annam or matter cannot explain the phenomena of life. It cannot, in fact, explain that which the physical sciences call force, without which matter cannot exist. And the first obvious manifestation of this force, in our experience, is the phenomena of life. Bhrigu thus arrived, next, at what may be called the Biological hypothesis and proclaimed Brahman or the First Cause or Ultimate

Reality as Pranam or the Life Principle. Gradually from Biology he rose to Psychology and declared Manas or the Intellect to be the Brahman. From Psychology he advanced to Metaphysics, and in the Unity of Self-consciousness or Bijnanam, he found his Brahman. There was, however, one great order of our experience which was not covered by any of these different hypotheses. That was the æsthetic or the emotional order, what is called Anandam in the Upanishads and which may be called pleasure, happiness, joy, love, or bliss in the English language. And Bhrigu finally declared that this Anandam is Brahman. The conclusion thus became absolutely irresistible, that Brahman or the First Cause —or the Ultimate Reality or the Absolute, is not absolutely Unknown and Unknowable, but that though beyond our knowledge *as an object,* this Absolute is known to us *as the condition* of all knowing, and becomes cognisible by us, through our own initimate and immediate experience, as subject.—as *Sat-Chit-Anandam.* In other words, we know the Absolute, through direct cognition as That Which Exists *by* Itself, is Conscious *of* Itself, and is Happy or Blessed *in* Itself. It depends on nothing else for It's existence, It's consciousness, It's happiness, or self-realisation. But all these, self-existence, self-consciousness, and self-blessedness or self-realisation, are characteristics of our own Self also, as we know it in our own immediate experience. Consequently, while the Brahman or the Absolute cannot be known *as an object.* It can be apprehended, in its very nature and essence, by the Self or the Subject, in the terms of its own immediate experience of itself. The Self and the Brahman are essentially one. Both are Infinite, Eternal, Universal. Neither admit of any real division or differentiation within itself. And this Upanishadic doctrine of the Self or the Absolute, as without any note or mark or division or differentiation within itself, the doctrine, that is, of the Nirguna Brahman, while it is almost infinitely deeper than the Spencerian doctrine of the Unknown and the Unknowable,—really offers no fundamental contradiction to it, and is not absolutely impossible of being, in a way, even reconciled with it. The transition from the agnosticism of Spencer to the gnosticism of the Upanishads, despite their mutual formal contradictions, is therefore neither impossible nor violent. The teachings of the Upanishads, therefore, did not really help to destroy but simply to fulfill, the earlier rationalism and agnosticism of Mrs. Besant.

NOT AN "ATHEIST" BUT "A NASTIKA"

In fact, people who have hitherto judged Mrs. Besant's conversion first from the Church of England Christianity to the atheism and secularism of the school of Charles Bradlaugh, and secondly from this atheism and secularism to the Theosophical thought of Madame Blavatsky and from this Theosophy finally to Hinduism, and have found in these changes a proof of the instability of her mental character and constitution, have forgotten or ignored the fact that those generalisations cover a very wide field, and there may be, and, indeed, are, the widest conceivable differences between one atheist and another, as there are between one theist and another. Every individual has his own definitions of these terms, and what may be called theism by one may be called atheism by another. Our ancients seem to have given a more rational definition of what is called atheism now, than is found in European thought. Their word was *nastika,* which did not mean one who denied a Personal God or Isvara, but one who refused to accept the possibility of the Unseen or the Super-sensuous. Those who said that there is nothing beyond what is cognised by the senses and the *manas* or the intellect, were called *nastikas* in one ancient lexicon; and those who accepted the possibility of the Unseen or the Super-sensuous were called *astikas.* The followers of the Sankhya did not accept God or Iswara, but they believed in the Unseen, and accepted the evidential value of the Vedas, which dealt with super-sensuous realities; they were, therefore, never classified with *nastikas,* but were simply called *niriswaras.* The only *nastikas* in our ancient thought were the *Charbakas* or *Lakayalas,* who denied the truth of the Unseen, and accepted no proof except that of the senses and the deductions and inductions based upon sense-testimony, as valid.

NASTIKA BY NATURE AND NASTIKA BY CIRCUMSTANCE

This denial of the Unseen or the Supersensuous may, again, be due to two reasons. There may be some people who are so constituted that they cannot, for the very life of them, honestly accept any evidence of the Unseen. There may be, indeed are, others whose inability to accept the reality of the Unseen is not due to their inherent incapacity to believe in it, but to the inadequacy of the evidence upon which they are asked to accept it. The former, adapting Lombroso's classification of criminals, may be called atheists or unbelievers or what would be called *nastikas* by our ancients,— by nature, or "instinctive atheists or *nastikas*;" and the latter atheists or *nastikas* from accidents of outer circumstances or environments,— "circumstantial atheists or *nastikas*." I have seen a few— though a very few people, indeed,—who are, by their very nature and constitution, absolutely incapable of conceiving the possibility of anything beyond and above what they cognise with their senses. These are "instinctive *nastikas*." I have seen others,—and their name is legion—who refuse to accept the existence of the Unseen, because of the obvious unreason of the grounds upon which they are asked to believe in it. These are "circumstantial *nastikas*," There are large numbers of men and women among this last class, who are, by their nature and constitution, capable of great and world-compelling Faith; but whose hereditary religious associations, or the currents of religious thought and life about whom, seem to them to be so outrageously irrational or unjust that they are driven by this rampant unreason and injustice, to deny not their own particular traditional faith only, but *all* faiths, summarily. This happens most frequently among people who have been trained to believe from their infancy that there is and can be nothing higher than their national religion and superior to the culture of their own country or race. This conceit of superior thought and civilisation of the European peoples, is far more responsible for the total denial of *all* religions by the Western sceptic, than the demands of his reason or the spirit of the positive sciences which dominates that reason to-day. They are atheists and sceptics *by circumstance* and not *by nature.*

MRS. BESANT'S POWER OF FAITH

Mrs. Besant was, in her youth an atheist and sceptic by reason of the peculiar environments and conditions of the religious thought and life of her people; and not by force of her inner nature. Nature did not make her a sceptic or unbeliever. Those whom Nature makes sceptics and unbelievers are woven with coarser fibres. She never endows these creations of hers with higher sensibilities and superior powers of imagination. And not even the most unfriendly critic of Mrs. Besant can deny her these superior spiritual endowments.

A born sceptic would not only have repudiated the authority of the established church or current religious faiths, but would have, equally, repudiated all ethical obligations also. There was nothing, indeed, in the philosophy of her youthful scepticism and secularism, to restrain Mrs. Besant from breaking away from all ethical restraints. But while her *opinions* freed her from these restraints, her Spirit and Nature, held her on to these, perhaps the more strongly and tenaciously, for this very outer intellectual repudiation of these moral obligations. And this very Purity of her life proves, at least to me, her superior spiritual make and constitution. Sceptics fashioned by Nature's own hand, those who are constitutionally incapable of believing in the Unseen or the Super-sensuous, are born rebels. They can never follow the duties of their traditional religions, even in their unreflective boyhood or girlhood, much less in their youth, with that wholehearted devotion with which Mrs. Besant sought to discharge her Christian duties, as long as she was inside the Christian Church. Her early faith in Christianity was by no means less sincere or ardent or soulful than her so-called atheistic and secularistic convictions, or her subsequent faith in the so-called super-naturalism of the Theosophic cult. While the objects of her faith or conviction have changed, with the changes in her intellectual and social outlook and environments, the Power of that Faith has always, really, remained the same. And it is this Power of Faith, this inherent and natural capacity to believe in the Unseen and the Super-sensuous, in whatever terms this Unseen may be expressed or presented to one's intellect,—which proves the inner and real character of one's spiritual nature and endowments. It is this inner and real character of a person's mind and soul which determines and explains his or her outer life and evolution. And Mrs. Besant's superior and fine-fibred mentality furnishes us with the true master-key of her changeful life.

ATHEISTIC IDEALS

Faith is "evidence of things unseen, and expectation of things hoped for." And judged by this definition, Mrs. Besant's so-called "Atheism" had greater "faith" than all the religions in Christendom. This "evidence" is furnished by our capacity to idealise,—to see the Ideal, which is unseen, in and through the real, which is seen. We find this evidence of Mrs. Besant's inborn "faith" in her maidenly romance for "the most sweet "Jesu Christ" fairer than the sons of men" whom somewhat after the manner of Madame Guion, she idealised or idealised as her beloved spouse. Subsequently, in her wild "atheistic" days, we find a no less strong proof of this "faith," in her view or vision of Man. Man to this reputed atheistic woman, was not a mere bundle of flesh, a despicable earth-worm, born to creep through mire and misery and end his days at last in the agony of death. This was the man as we find him in the mass, and see him in our actual sense-experience. But Mrs. Besant's Ideal Man, for whom she laboured and wrought, fighting the thousand and one enemies of human progress and human happiness, that hold him down under their heels, was, in her atheistic days, as I think, he is even to-day,— "In form strong and fair, perfect in physical development as the Hercules in Grecian art, radiant in love, glorious in self-reliant power with lips bent firm to resist oppression, and melt into curves of passion and of pity; with deep farseeing eyes, gazing piercingly into the secrets of the unknown, and resting lovingly on the beauties around him; with hands strong to work in the present, with heart full of hope which the future shall realise, making earth glad with his labour and beautiful with his skill." (Gospel of Atheism—1876; Quoted in Autobiography).

"This, this," as she has herself told us, was the Ideal Man "enshrined in her atheistic heart." And one of the reasons of her revolt against religion as she saw it preached and practised about her, was the ill-concealed contempt in which it held man as man, whatever fancies it might weave around him as soul or spirit. Contrasting her own ideal of man with that of Christianity, labouring under mediaeval abstractions, she declared :—

"The ideal humanity of the Christian is the humanity of the slave, poor, meek, broken-spirited, humble, submissive to authority, however oppressive and unjust; the ideal humanity of the atheist is the humanity of the freeman who knows no lord, who brooks no tyranny, who relies on his own strength, who makes his brother's quarrel his, proud, true-hearted, loyal brave." *Ibid.*

True it is that all through her early "atheistic" days, Mrs. Besant refused to go beyond the seen, the material, and the real, and would accept nothing unless established by positive scientific evidence. Yet, all the same, she was constantly pointing to the unseen, the ideal, what may in fact be even called intuitive and spiritual, in her vigorous fights with popular theistic ideas and superstitions. Replying to the charge that she was "taking away all beauty out of human life, all hope, all warmth, all inspiration;" by her denial of God and soul, and giving us "cold duty for filial obedience, and inexorable, laws in the place of God," —she cried out:—

"All beauty from life ?" Is there, then, no beauty in the idea of forming part of the great life of the universe, no beauty in conscious harmony with Nature, no beauty in faithful service, no beauty in deals of every virtue ? "All hope ?" Why, I give you more than hope, I give you certainty : if I bid you labour for this world, it is with the knowledge that this world will repay you a thousandfold, because society will grow purer, freedom more settled, law more honoured' life more full and glad. What is your heaven ? A heaven in the clouds! I point to a heaven attainable on earth. "All warmth?" What! you serve warmly a God unknown and invisible, in a sense, the projected shadow of your own imaginings, and can only serve coldly your brother whom you see at your side ? There is no warmth in brightening the lot of the sad, in reforming abuses, in establishing equal justice for rich and poor? You find warmth in the church, but none in the home ? Warmth in imagining the cloud glories of heaven, but none in creating substantial glories on earth? "All inspiration?" If you want inspiration to feeling, to sentiment, perhaps you had better keep to your Bible and your creeds if you want inspiration to work, go and walk through the East of London, or the back streets of Manchester. You are inspired to tenderness as you gaze at the wounds of Jesus dead in Judaua long ago, and find no inspiration in the wounds of men and women, dying in the England of to-day? You "have tears to shed for Him," hut none for the sufferer at your doors ? His passion arouses our sympathies, but you see no pathos in the passion of the poor ? "Duty colder than filial obedience ?" What do you mean by filial obedience ? Obedience to your ideal of goodness and love—is it not so ? Then how is duty cold ?

I offer you ideals for your homage : here is Truth for your Mistress, to whose exaltation you shall devote your intellect; here is Freedom for your General for whose triumph you shall fight; here is Love for your Inspirer, who shall influence your every thought; here is Man for your Master—not in heaven, but on earth—to whose service you shall consecrate every faculty of your being.

"Inexorable law in the place of God ?" Yes; a stern certainty that you shall not waste your life, yet gather a rich reward at the close : that you shall not sow misery, yet reap gladness; that you shall not be selfish, yet be crowned with love nor shall you sin, yet find safety in repentance. True, our creed *is* a stern one, stern with the sternness of Nature. But if we be in the right, look to yourselves; laws do not check their action for your ignorance; fire will not cease to scorch, because you "did not know." *(On the Nature and Existence of God*—1874 Quoted in Autobiography).

Those who knew the true meaning and character of Faith, will not fail therefore, to recognise what a large fund of this Faith there was in this strange, and impetuous and soulful woman, who rose up in arms against the current faiths of her people because these had no foundations and no outlook into the ideal of human grandeur and human glory. Here too, in this last article of Mrs. Besant's so called atheistic creed we discover the deep affinities between her view of Law, and the doctrine of Karma which from the very first formed so vital a part of Theosophic Ethics.

Mrs. Besant's natural and inborn capacity to not only idealise the actual, but also to feel an inner assurance of the realisation of all our highest hopes, in some shape or another is equally seen in her "atheistic" views of "immortality." "Is it true that Atheism has no immortality ?" she asks, and answers:—

"What is immortality? Is Beetheven's true immortality in his continued personal consciousness, or in his glorious music deathless while the world endures ? Is Shelly's true life in his existence in some far-off heaven, or in pulsing liberty his lyrics send through men's heart, when they respond to the strains of his lyre. Music does not die, though the brain be shivered; love does not die, though one's heart-strings be rent; and no great thinker dies so long as his thought re-echoes through the ages, its melody the fuller-toned the more human brains send its music on. Not only to the hero and the sage is this immortality given; it belongs to each according to the measure of his deeds; worldwide life for world-wide service; straitened life for straitened work; each according as he sows, and the harvest is gathered by each in his rightful order." (*Gospel of Atheism).*

If faith be, as St. Paul defined it, "the evidence of things unseen and expectation of things hoped for," then, it can hardly be denied that in these passionate confessions of her very atheistical faiths, this youthful idealist gave much stronger evidence of this faith than we find in all the pious professions of churchmen and evangelicals." We see in these atheistic writings of Mrs. Besant a very clear and convincing explanation of her subsequent conversion from the secularism of the school of Charles Braudlaugh to the Theosophy of Madame Blavatsky.

"FROM STORM TO PEACE"

In Hinduism, however, she found, it seems to me, a much fuller reconciliation between her earlier ideals and her new illuminations, than she had found even in the theology of Madame Blavatsky. Indeed, the strange spell which the latter cast upon her, was far more personal and hypnotic than anything else. I had never come in personal contact with Madame Blavatsky, but I have heard from friends who had seen her face to face, that she exercised a strong and mysterious power over all who went near her. It was not so much her thought, her philosophy, or even her conversations, though she was undoubtedly a woman of great intellectual power and a finished and versatile conversationalist,—as her mere presence which so strangely fascinated those who went near her. It happened in the case of Mrs. Besant also. Mrs. Besant was then passing through a period of severe intellectual and moral stress and strain. She had already found out, with larger experience and deeper analysis of the facts of life, the limitations of her earlier philosophy of life.

Her noble idealism and consecrated service of man had led her to take up all sorts of social work. She had thrown herself heart and soul into the great reform movements of the day. She had gradually drifted into Socialism and had been writing, speaking, organising, fighting day and night, against the economic slavery of the English proletariat. This brought her in contact with the very heart and soul of the labouring classes. And all these experiences commenced, at first unconsciously to herself, to undermine the basis of her earlier opinions and convictions. This feeling of failure commenced to gnaw into her ideals and sorely wound her tender susceptibilities. She commenced to increasingly feel that "something more than I had was needed for the cure of the social ills. The Socialist position sufficed on the economic side, but where to gain the inspiration, the motive, which should lead to the realisation of the Brotherhood of Man ?" She found it impossible to organise bands of workers. "There was not a real movement of self-sacrificing devotion, in which men worked for Love's sake only, and asked but to give and not to take. Where was the material for the nobler social order, where the hewn stones for the building of the Temple of Man ? A great despair would oppress me as I sought for such a movement and found it not."

Not only this; but there had also been slowly growing a conviction, since 1886, as she says, that her "philosophy of life was not sufficient; that life and mind were other than, more than, she had dreamed." All these had thrown her into a fresh intellectual and moral struggle. It was in the midst of this struggle—storm, as she herself calls it,—that Mrs. Besant first came across Madame Blavatsky's "Secret Doctrine" just published, and rose from its study with the glimpses of a new light in her mind's eye. From the book she went to its author; and at the very first visit was completely conquered by her strange, magnetic personality. Madame did not speak a word of Theosophy or occultism, worked no miracles, talked no mysteries. She talked like a "woman of the world chatting with her evening visitors." That was all—outwardly. But beneath all this the soul was speaking in its silent language to soul; and when the interview ended, Mrs. Besant rose to go,—

> "for a moment the veil lifted, and two brilliant, piercing eyes met mine, and with a yearning throb in the voice: "Oh, my dear Mrs. Besant, if you would only come among us!" I felt a well-nigh uncontrollable desire to bend down and kiss her, under the compulsion of that yearning voice, those compelling eyes,... (Autobiography).

The personal magnetism of "H. P. B." had, no doubt, a great deal to do with the conversion of Mrs. Besant to Theosophy; but she had been a seeker after something more than her so-called atheism and materialism offered, for a long time previous to it. Nor was the "Secret Doctrine," her first acquaintance with Occultism. She had studied the new Psychology which "was advancing with strides," and was slowly removing the older and impassable gulf between mind and body. She had studied "the obscurer sides of consciousness dreams, hallucinations, illusions, insanity." "Into the darkness shot a ray of light—A. P. Sinnet's "Occult World," with its wonderfully suggestive letters, expounding not the supernatural but a nature under law, wider than I had dared to conceive." The phenomena of clairvoyance, clair-audience, thought-reading, she found to be real.

Under all the rush of the outer life, already sketched, these questions were working in my mind, their answers were being diligently sought. I read a variety of books, but could find little in them that satisfied me. I experimented in various ways suggested in them, and got some (to me) curious results. I finally convinced myself that there was some hidden thing, some hidden power, and resolved to seek until I found, and by the early spring of 1889, I had grown desperately determined to find, at all hazards, what I sought. At last, sitting alone in deep thought as I had become accustomed to do after the sun had set, filled with an intense but nearly hopeless longing to solve the riddle of life and mind, I heard a voice that was later to become to me the holiest sound on earth, bidding me take courage for the light was near. A fortnight passed, and then Mr. Stead gave into my hands two large volumes. "Can you review these? My young men all fight shy of thorn, but you are quite mad enough on these subjects to make something of them." I took the books; they were the two volumes of "The Secret Doctrine," written by H. P. Blavatsky. (Autobiography).

And when we read all this "previous history," we find nothing inexplicable, nothing unnatural, nothing that can be described as a sudden leap into the unknown, or a revolutionary somersault, in the conversion of Mrs. Besant from Free thought to Theosophy. On the contrary, one plainly sees in it, only a gradual and natural evolution of her older materialism into a kind of spirituality which did not base itself upon anything that might be called a contradiction of the material explanation of the universe, but what was only an expansion and fulfilment of it.

FROM OCCULTISM TO HINDUISM

Mrs. Besant had denied the Unseen of popular Christianity, because it set itself over against the seen. She had refused to accept a God who stood apart from the world, who was everything that the world was not who was a contradiction of actual experience as we gain it through our senses, and not an explanation of it. Christianity had failed to bridge the gulf between mind and body, between spirit and matter, between the Unseen and the seen, to Mrs. Besant. It was this self-contradictory dualism of popular, and particularly, Protestant Christian theology, that had driven her away from the Christian Communion. But even in her so-called atheistic days, she had never, for a moment, lost hold of her inner conviction of the fundamental unity of the universe. Matter and Mind were to her not two entities but different modes of one and the same substance. But matter being more readily cognisable by our outer senses, she had embraced a material philosophy of the universe, rejecting the so-called spiritual philosophies of Christendom, which could not explain the organic relation between spirit and matter. But if the spiritual philosophy of Christianity failed to explain the facts of our material life, even so, Mrs. Besant gradually found out, as others had done both before and after her, that her own material hypothesis also failed equally to explain the subtler and hidden phenomena of the mental world, that are summed up by the term "Occult." In Madame Blavatsky's Theosophy the emphasis of which was unmistakably more on the occult than on what would be called truly spiritual at least in our own ancient thought and language, Mrs. Besant found a bridge between matter and mind. Here she saw, almost like Bhrigu, that while matter could not interpret the mind, the mind could, demonstrably, interpret matter. Her first step from Materialism to Theosoophy, was thus, it seems to me, an advance from the Anna-Brahman to the Prana-Brahman of Bhrigu, of the Bhrigu-Baruni episode of the Taittiriya Upanishad referred to above. From this her transition first to the sublime theosophy of the Upanishads, and from it, finally, to the Spiritual monism of the Hindu thought, was both rapid and easy.

WHAT SHE HAS FOUND IN HINDUISM

Here in Hinduism, Mrs. Besant found a professedly religious system which did not in any way seek to interfere with the freedom of individual reason or conscience. It was a religion without a creed. It accepted all; each according to his own stage of development. It left each man free to follow the innermost promptings of his individual nature, believe or refuse to believe just as that nature commanded. It rejected none. The theist who believed in a personal God; the pantheist who repudiated this Personality; the Unitarian or *Ekantin,* who believed in one God only; the so-called polytheist, who believed in many gods; the follower of the way of *Jnanam* who worshipped in spirit, and the follower of the way of *Karma,* who worshipped through outer rituals and sacrifices; the *Yogin* who followed the way of meditation; the *Karmin,* who sought God and salvation through service of man or *laka-shreya*; those who blindly followed the law; and those who obeyed no Law except that of their inner Nature and Life,—the highest *Sannyasin* and Paramhansa :— all these were included in the Hindu communion. The Ritualists or *Jajnikas* of the school of Jaimini, were practically "atheists"—in the European sense of the term.—they did not believe in the existence of God or gods, but only proclaimed the unseen and mysterious power of the Vedic *mantras* and ceremonies, to produce their promised fruits; the *Sunkhyas* who proclaimed that there was no proof of the existence of Iswara or the Lord; the *Naiyayikas* or Logicians, who are dualists; the Vedantists who are Monists,—and even the *Vaisheshikas* who believe in the eternity of matter and may, therefore, be classed with the materialists;—all these have a place in Hindu thought and religion. They are all Hindus. They are all left free to beat their own music out, to work their own way to the Ultimate Goal. Unity in Diversity; Freedom through Subjection; Universality built upon Individuality; the Ideal built upon the Real; and God enthroned not outside the world but in every part and particle of it, and revealed in Man, in the measure of his own human perfection :—all these completely harmonised with the whole intellectual and moral nature of Mrs. Besant. Madame Blavatsky's Occultism had introduced her into the Realm of the Unknown, and had indicated the Endless Possibilities of the human mind. Hinduism introduced her into the Supreme actualities of the Realm of the Spirit, where all matter is seen in their spiritual essences and all man is found in their Divine Perfection. Here was the "Temple of Man" which she had been seeking to build throughout her struggling days with Mr. Charles Bradlaugh and the Socialists or the Fabians; but it was a Temple which was also the Temple of God, for here God and Man are One.

It is thus found that if Mrs. Besant has very materially helped to rehabilitate our national religion to thousands of our English-educated country-men by her interpretations of ancient Hindu wisdom, this Hinduism itself has also helped to make her own life and philosophy deeper and fuller than what her earlier lessons in Theosophy and

Occultism had been able to do. Col. Olcott and Madame Blavatsky had built up their Theosophy upon Buddhistic Agnosticism and psycho-physics. Mrs. Besant has brought Theosophy into line with the spiritual philosophy of Vedantic gnosticism. Above all, she has lent an element of Bhakti or Emotion which had before been wanting in the Theosophic cult and culture. The emphasis of Theosophy was at first on Occultism, next it was on the Agnosticism of the earlier Upanishads and Buddhistic metaphysics; then it was transferred, mainly under Mrs. Besant to Vedantic Gnosticism or Brahma-Jnana and the Way of Works of the Bhagavad-Geeta. To-day we find an increasing emphasis on the Bhagavata or Bhakti Schools. And though I cannot say, how far, this is directly due to Mrs. Besant, we all know that she started the filiation of Theosophie thought and culture with the whole Hindu system, Vedic Upanishadic and Pauranic, but for which Theosophy could not advance to the thresh-hold of this, the highest achievement of Hinduism, attained through different Vaishnavic cults and cultures.

A MISSIONARY TO THE HINDUS

From her secularistic and socialistic work in Britain Mrs. Besant came to this country, about a couple of years after the passing away of Madame Blavatsky, when the mantle of that great teacher fell practically upon her, as a Theosophical Missionary to the Hindus. Frankly speaking, we who belonged to what claimed to represent the advanced wing of modern thought and life in India, did not quite like this new white missionary among us. Apart from all theological differences, many of us who had imbibed the new National Spirit and had commenced to feel the first quickening of a new National Self-Consciousness within us, could not easily reconcile ourselves to this new phase of foreign domination. What right, we asked, had this lady from England to pose as a teacher of higher Hindu thought? We better liked and appreciated some other European and American ladies who came a few days later to us, not as teachers but as pupils, not as the high priestess of our own ancient wisdom, but as humble learners and workers for our country. But though we did not like Mrs. Besant's apostolic activities in those early days, none but the most blind partisan can, looking back upon the results of her labours in this country extending over nearly a quarter of a century, refuse to recognise the valuable services which she has rendered to the cause of the religious, the moral, the social, and lastly, of the political advancement of the Indian people.

Nor is it very difficult, now that all contemporary controversies and conflicts have been finally set at rest, to recognise the inner impulses that must have driven her to take up this missionary work. True it is that Mrs. Besant found the final solution of all her lifelong problems in what may, well be described as higher Hindu thought. The gospel of human freedom; the synthesis between what are called God. Flesh, and the World; the recognition of the three-fold ways or disciplines, namely, the way of jnana or gnosis, of karma or works, and bhakti or love and faith, through which the final Illumination or Emancipation could be equally reached; the staggering declaration of the fundamental Divinity of Man; the explanation of all ills, whether physical, mental, or spiritual, not as punishments for man's sins, personal and original, but as the fruits of his own karma, and as incidents of the evolutionary process through which he gradually rises from the lowest to the highest planes of existence, finally reaching perfect and conscious unity with the Universal; all these fitted in with the fundamental philosophy of her life. In all these, as I have already said, she found not a repudiation but only a correction, not a destruction but only a fulfilment of her earlier ideals and aspirations. In this ancient Hindu Idealism she found the full revelation of the inner light that had been guiding her steps onward ever since her girlhood, from her beautiful romantic faith, through her youthful rational doubt, and the toils and tribulations of her selfless work for the uplift of down-trodden humanity, until she reached the haven of Theosophy, with its philosophy of Nature and Man bound together in one chain of mind substance and mind evolution. This Theosophy placed in her hands the master key to the invaluable treasures of ancient Hindu wisdom. But alas ! what a sad, what a wide, wide gulf did she find between those glorious idealities and the inglorious actualities of present day Hindu life and thought!

Mrs. Besant's so-called atheistical and materialistic philosophy had done one great service to her mental life and character. It had supplied a much-needed corrective to the inborn idealism and exuberant imaginativeness of her highly sensitive soul. It gave her a grip of life's stern actualities which could not be idealised or etherialised away by any amount of sympathy or appreciation, by any kind of conjuring tricks which might call up the hidden potencies or beauties of our actual work-a-day life. She was not made to play blind man's buff with the realities of life and world about her. Had she found it possible to continue her life as she had begun it, and spend her days as the kind but comfortable wife of a Church dignitary, helping the poor, comforting the lonely, soothing the grief-worn with the dreams of the life to come, and airily dismissing all human sufferings as a dispensation of an inscrutable Providence,— it might have been different. If she had become a convert to Hinduism directly she had been landed in her rational doubts regarding the Christian dogmas, or had taken to it as the latest fashionable fad, seeking to go through yogic practices with upturned eyes and poetic pose), and indulge in all sorts of talks about the "whichness of the why" and "the whyness of the which;" she might have fallen an easy prey to the superbly sentimental subjectivism of mediaeval Hindu thought, and might have failed, in her idealisation, to realise the cruel actualities of present day Hindu life and institutions. But she had received her baptism in the truths and actualities of human sorrow and sin in the slums of London and Manchester. Life as it was seen, was too real, too stern, too cruel, too full of falsehoods and brutalities to her, to be airily conjured away and replaced by fairy fancies of the ideal world. Mrs. Besant was too strong a realist still, too sane an idealist, too long used to take a scientific view of life, to overlook these actualities. And it seems to me that it was this cruel disparity between our glorious ideals and our inglorious lives which impelled her to transfer her field of educational and reform activities from England to India, and take up the mission work of the Theosophical Society among the Hindus.

MRS. BESANT'S MISSIONARY METHODS

And she adopted the same principles and methods, *mutatis mutandis,* which she had pursued in her own homeland, in all her educational and reform work among her own people. She went about among the lowliest and poorest classes of British society as one of them. She did not relieve their sufferings from outside and above, but tried to teach the poor and the down-trodden to rise themselves by their own efforts, out of their poverty and degradation. And in all this, her first and foremost care was to lead these people to know themselves, to realise that they too are human, fully endowed with all the rights and having all the possibilities of common humanity. Self-respect and self-reliance were the two fundamental principles of her missionary labours among the British poor. She could not, therefore, bear with the "charitable" ways of the Christian philanthropists. "Christian charity ?" she cried out: "We know its work. It gives a hundredweight of coal and five pounds of beef once a year to a family whose head could earn a hundred such doles if Christian justice allowed him fair wage for the work he performs. It plunders the workers of the wealth they make, and then flings back at them a thousandth part of their own product as "charity." It builds hospitals for the poor whom it has poisoned in filthy courts and alleys and workhouses for the wornout creatures from whom it has wrung every energy, every hope, every joy. "Miss Cobbe summons us to admire Christian civilisation, and we see idlers flaunting in the robes woven by the toilers, a glittering tinselled superstructure, founded on the tears, the strugglings, the grey, hopeless misery of the poor." The picture is no doubt one-sided, and overdrawn. These are not all nor the most prominent aspects of Christian civilisation, as Mrs. Besant will herself frankly admit to-day. But it was the out-cry of her pitiful soul weighted down with the scenes of suffering and wrong about her. And in her crusade against these her first attempt always was to rouse the poor and the downtrodden themselves to a sense of their own power and possibility. For this, she had, of necessity, to rouse the indignation of the poor and helpless against the wrongs which they have hitherto suffered in silence.

And the main motive was to inspire them with confidence in themselves.

And it seems to me that she followed the same methods, and exactly from the self-same motives, in her early missionary work among us. She saw that educated India had lost faith in itself. The Hindus had no faith not only in their ancient or mediaeval dogmas and doctrines, which might have been a matter of little moment under other circumstances, but that they had lost all faith in their own powers and possibilities. They felt the indignity of their position, but had not the courage and the strength to boldly and manfully amend or end it. They assumed a more or less apologetic tone in the presence of the foreigner, and seemed to have been weighted down with a sense of their national impotence and inferiority. The Hindu revival of the eighties of the last century had, no doubt commenced to quicken in the people a new consciousness of their superiority. But this was too imaginary to touch the actualities of the present. It was too subjective in its ideals, too mediaeval in its out-look, too hidebound in its practice. It was a glorification of the past at the expense of the present. It declared war against European Christian agressions, no doubt, but roused little practical enthusiasm for uplift either of the individual or of society, even after its own ancient or mediaeval ideals. Above all this Revival practically denied the need of the reform and readjustment of present life and manners to help the realisation of our high national destiny. Indeed, it had a very feeble vision of this destiny, and no consciousness of the great mission which we have among the peoples of the modern world a mission not lesser but distinctly greater than what our forefathers discharged among the ancients.

Mrs. Besant came and took up the work where the Hindu Revival had practically left it. The Hindu Revival, as its name implied, sought to *revive.* Hindu faiths and ideals; and the faiths and ideals which it sought to revive, were not of the earliest Upanishadic times, nor even of the times of the Mahabharata, but practically of the later and decidedly mediaeval period, the period that followed the decline and the final disappearance of Buddhism from the country and the rise of the neo-Hinduism dominated by the abstractions of Sankara-Vedantic thought, and by the ritualism and symbolism that rose along with it, out of the poetry and imagery of the Puranas and by the revived rigidities of caste exclusiveness and the resuscitated domination of the Brahmins which is an inevitable concommitant of all supernaturalism in religion. The symbolic deities and the Brahmins go hand in hand; the one cannot, at least in popular Hindu ceremonialism, get on without the other. When, particularly, the symbol is not a natural representation of the thing or person or power it symbolises, but is an arbitrary and artificial thing, bearing no reasonable affinity or association with its original, and when, consequently, this relation has to be conjured up, by some magical processes as that which is known as Prana-Pratishtha or the investing the symbol with the life and presence of the deity, which is a universal element of all so-called idolatry in Hinduism, the priestly function becomes then an essential feature of this kind of ritualism, and the priestly pretensions are sought to be supported by it in a vareity of ways. The Hindu Revival sought to recreate people's faith in this mediaeval Hinduism and thus tried to re-establish the social supremacy of the Brahminical caste which had considerably been weakened under the influence of modern ideas and the conditions of modern life.

Mrs. Besant did not openly go against this Revival, on the contrary, she seemed to support it, in her earlier missionary activities among us. But in so doing she tried to give not only some sort of a rational interpretation to our ancient faiths and current practices, but at the same time, by the very fact that she whose claims to teachership of religion could never be tolerated, strictly speaking, by Hindu orthodoxy, was accepted as an interpreter of Hindu sastras, her propaganda helped unconsciously to bread on the basis of this very Hindu Revival. The legend of her previous birth as a pure Brahmin, could not explain away this open outrage on Hindu orthodoxy. For, the soul has no caste, it is neither Brahmin nor Sudra, neither black nor white, neither sinful nor virtuous. The Soul is eternally pure, eternally self-illumined, eternally emancipated. This is the universal teaching of Hinduism. Brahminhood or Sudrahood, these are accidents of the outer temporal life, and have concern with the soul's present incarnation only. So, strictly speaking, this legend of Mrs. Besant's previous Brahminical caste or heredity, did not remove the taint of her present non-Brahminhood. The way that she was welcomed by Hindu orthodoxy as a powerful champion of its cause, went very far, therefore, in its practical effect, to braaden and liberalise the Hindu Revival Movement to which she at first lent considerable support. And the principal result of it was the creation of a new self-consciousness and self-confidence, the birth of a new and aggressive spirit of self-assertion and the rapid growth of a universal outlook, which drove the mind of the Hindu people to visions of world conquest. And this prospect of the moral and spiritual conquest of the modern world, including their British conquerors, worked as a mighty set off against the sense of their political impotence.

THEOSOPHY AND POLITICS

From the very beginning of its activities in India, the Theosophical Society had not only disclaimed all political motives, but had always scrupulously avoided even the least semblance of sympathy or association with the political agitations of the educated classes. This policy was forced upon the Theosophic founders by the fact of their non-British nationality. There was not much love or fraternisation in those days between England and America. Indeed, up to the outbreak of the Spanish American war, in the last decade of the last century, the memories of the conflict between England and the American Colonies that ultimately led to the independence of these Colonies, rankled in the American heart. This feeling of antagonism was pretty strong, on both sides, in the seventies and eighties of the nineteenth century, when the founders of the Theosophical Society first came among us. The relations of great Britain with Russia was much worse. The scare of a Russian invasion of India was then at its very height. And the fact that Colonel Olcott was an American citizen, and his associate, Madame Blavatsky was Russian by birth, naturally aroused considerable suspicion in the official mind in India. They had, therefore, to work very cautiously to live this suspicion down. This explains the dissociation of the Theosophical Movement in India from all political activities among our educated classes, however reasonable, lawful, and constitutional these might be.

But though without any open political association or reference, the indirect effect of the Theosophical teaching upon our general political consciousness and inspiration was not at all insignificant.

Theosophy proclaimed the superior moral and spiritual inheritance of our people. It declared that as descendants of the ancient Hindu sages and saints, we still had a much superior spiritual nature than the recently-humanised races of the West. It proclaimed that even in our present degradations, we were a much finer-fibred people than the Europeans. And it called us to all these high inheritance of our past, by claiming and reacquiring which, we might once more be the teachers of humanity even as our ancient forefathers had been. All these inevitably woke up a new pride of race in us, and thus laid the foundations of that racial conflict and competition which subsequently became such a powerful and prominent element of our new political life.

Though scrupulously avoiding all public associations with political activities in the country, the Theosophical Movement contributed, in this indirect way, no mean inspiration to our present political life and aspirations. Indeed, the Theosophical leaders have openly claimed, if I remember rightly, the actual fathership of the Indian National Congress. The late Mr. Allan O. Hume, who is justly called the Father of the National Congress, was a Theosophist; and it is impossible to deny that we owe to the teachings of Theosophy the acquisition of so distinguished a member of the Indian Civil Service, to the rank of our political leaders. There were many others also, who considerably helped at the inauguration of the Congress movement, who were prominent Theosophists. The late Mr. Narendra Nath Sen, editor of the *Indian Mirror,* which was in those days a most outspoken and powerful exponent of popular rights and liberties and uncompromising critic of the Indian Bureaucracy, was a leader of Theosophy in his time. Sir Subramanya Iyer at that time a leader of the High Court Bar in Madras, was another prominent Theosophist, who had considerable influence over the educated public of the Southern Presidency. There were a few others, I think, who were identified with the Theosophical movement in their respective localities, who met during Christmas, 1885, in Bombay, at the First Indian National Congress. Apart from this, it is said that the idea of the Congress was first mooted the previous year, in December 1884, at a meeting of the leading delegates to the Theosophical Convention and some friends and sympathisers of that movement who had been present at the Convention, who gathered at the house of Dewan

Bahadur Raghunath Rao, after the Convention was over, and laid down plans for convening the great National assembly. Of course other forces had also been at work, tending towards the same goal. The Indian Association of Calcutta, which originally started with an all-India programme, and sought to cover the whole continent with a regular net-work of political organisations with the object of laying down the foundations of the future National Parliament of India, had, in fact, convened a National Conference in Calcutta about the same time when the First Congress was sitting in Bombay. There were other organisations also working towards the same end. But it will have to be conceded, I think, that the Theosophic Convention was the first all-India organisation among us; and consequently, the Theosophic leaders who were free to take up political work found it easier to help the organisation of the Congress than it would have been found by them. But while some of the most prominent Indian leaders of the Theosophical Movement joined the Congress, following Mr. Hume, the founders of the Theosophical Society, as well the Society itself, carefully kept up its non-political character, which has been fully maintained by it up to this day.

PROM RELIGIOUS PROPAGANDISM TO EDUCATIONAL ACTIVITIES

When Mrs. Besant came into the leadership of the Theosophical Movement, upon the demise of Madame Blavatsky, and long before she became its official head after the death of its life-president Col. Olcott,— she had of necessity to keep up the old policy and attitude of political neutrality, even though the reasons that worked in the case of her predecessors did not exist for her. Her earlier propagandist activities were, therefore, confined exclusively to the religious and socio-religious field. But it did not take her very long to realise the difficulty of building up a real and sturdy religious or socio-religious idealism in the community and particularly to coin it into character, under the blighting influences which the existing system of officialised education created in the country. The defects of this education are many and universally recognised. The education which the Government schools and colleges impart is, for one thing, purely theoretic, and hardly touches the deeper springs of either the intellectual or the moral life of the pupils. These educational institutions are as something apart from the real life of the people, and are resorted to by them mainly, if not entirely, from mere economic motives, with the object of helping them to earn their daily bread. In the next place, this education is absolutely secular; the Government policy of religious neutrality preventing the introduction of any kind of religious instruction in its curricula. The exceedingly feeble bands that hold the pupils and the teachers together in these schools and colleges and the practical absence of all healthy social relations between them, and the utter disparity between the atmosphere of the school and the home, all these work very prejudicially to the growth of a healthy intellectual and moral life in the educated community. It is almost impossible for any earnest religious propaganda to produce its desired fruits upon a soil like this. This officialised education tends to make men selfish, life frivolous, and weaken the sense of all higher duties. Sound conviction is difficult to grow and vigorous and manly character—almost impossible to build up under these conditions.

While the Government Department of Public Instruction and the Government-controlled Universities were imparting this purely secular and exceedingly rootless education,—secular in the rather vulgar sense of the term, and not in the sense in which the principle of non-denominational education is sought to be enforced upon the British School Boards—the Government-aided schools and colleges in this country under Christian Missionary management, tried to force instruction in an alien religion upon unwilling pupils. This compulsory religious teaching did not receive the intellectual acceptance of the students, and was in most cases secretly resented by them, as a sheer waste of their time, and sometimes even as an insult to their own religion —to which they were compelled to submit from low pecuniary considerations only. This unpalatable and enforced religious teaching killed the very roots of faith and reverence in the pupils, and very seriously undermined frequently the native sensitiveness of their intellect to truth and their natural youthful enthusiasm for the higher ideals of life; and practically developed the soul-killing tendency to take a very vulgar and selfish view of life and duty. No idealism or superior spirituality could be reared upon an intellectual and moral soil like this.

Mrs. Besant seemed to have realised all this before she was long among us, seeking to preach Theosophic ideals to our educated countrymen. She saw that if the teachings of Theosophy, as she understood it, were to take root in this country in the life and thought of our rising generations, then means must be found to free the young hopefuls of the nation from the blighting influences of current methods and principles of Government and Missionary education. And as her principal propagandist work was carried on mainly among the educated Hindus, her first educational activities were naturally meant for Hindu youths. It was thus that she came to feel the need of a system of national education for the people of this country, as early as 1896; and the Central Hindu College at Benares was started by her "as a step in that direction."

But Mrs. Besant held then a somewhat subordinate position in the Theosophical organisation. She was not yet its official head. The political ardour of her Socialist and Fabian associations had also been thrown somewhat into the back-ground by the onrush of her new enthusiasm for the abstractions of her first Theosophical ideas. Occultism and the metaphysical idealism of Theosophic thought were then the strongest obsessions of her mind and the absorbing preoccupations of her missionary life.

She had only touched then, it seems to me, what may be best called the static side of Hinduism, and had still to seize its equally important dynamic side. Hinduism was to her then, practically, a department of "Ancient Wisdom" only, which while it was needed for the modern man, stood in little need itself of being "modernised," to meet modern requirements. The spirit of criticism that had from age to age refined even Hinduism and brought it into line with the highest thoughts and speculations, as well as with the urgent practical needs of the times, had yet to awaken in her. It was only natural, and almost inevitable indeed, for her, to accommodate the new education which she sought to impart in her Hindu College more to the outer forms of Hinduism than was really necessary to maintain the natural continuity of our national thought and life. The religious instruction which she introduced here was more traditional than rational, more mediaeval than modern. It was not, I am afraid, really scientific. In fact, it overlooked, in the selection of the Bhagavad-Geeta as a text book on religion,—for instance—the fundamental principle of "adhi-karce-bheda" or the regulation of religious and spiritual training by the inner qualifications of the pupils or disciples. But all these limitations notwithstanding, it must be acknowledged that Mrs. Besant's Central Hindu College sought to impart an education which, so far as the Hindu students were concerned, was immensely superior in many respects to that received by the students of the Government or Missionary institutions. In her Central Hindu College at Benares, to quote Mrs. Besant's own words,—"Englishmen and Indians worked together on equal terms, and love not fear controlled (the relations of teacher and pupil), mutual courtesy and respect were the rule of life, independence was wedded to good manners; the Englishman was loved as much as the Indian, patriotism walked hand in hand with loyalty, and T. R. M. the Prince and Princess of Wales needed no soldiers and no police to guard them, but were guarded by the boys themselves." All this is true : but the isolation in which Mrs. Besant was living then from the progressive political thoughts and activities of the country, prevented her Central Hindu College from realising the full and complete ideals of true National Education, as we have understood it for the last ten years and more.

MRS. BESANT AND THE NATIONALIST MOVEMENT IN BENGAL

This isolation from our political activities was, it seems to me, very largely responsible for the somewhat hostile attitude which she took up towards the Nationalist upheaval in Bengal during the years 1905 to 1907 and 1908 or 1909. There are people who have not been able to forget some of the incidents of those years, in which Mrs. Besant played a rather prominent part. Her chief interest in those days was centred in her Central Hindu College at Benares. And it was here that she first came into conflict with the new Nationalist enthusiasm in the country.

In 1905 the whole of Bengal rose up in a determined protest against the Partition of that Province by Lord Curzon, and, as a retaliatory measure for this wanton outrage upon nationalist sentiments, declared a boycott of British goods. The leaders of Bengal further declared that the 16th day of October, 1905, the Partition-Day, should be observed as a day of mourning by the Bengalee people. There were a good many Bengalee boys in Mrs. Besant's Central Hindu College School at Benares. And following the advice of the Bengal leaders, and the example of their compatriots in the home province, these boys decided to attend their classes in mourning dress. The Government Education Department in Bengal had taken up a very definite attitude of hostility to these demonstrations of nationalist feeling by the students of Government and Government-aided educational institutions. Students who went to their schools in mourning dress, that is, without their shoes—were expelled from their class, and heavily fined for this enforced absence. Mrs. Besant took up, practically, the same attitude in regard to this matter; and, though she did not inflict any fines upon those who participated in the Partition-Day celebrations, all the same she refused them admission to their classes, just as the Bengal officials of the Government educational institution had done.

In common fairness to Mrs. Besant, it must be admitted now, however difficult it may have been for us to recognise it in those exciting days,—that we who so strongly condemned her action in this matter, at that time, did not stop to calmly, consider the real psychology of her policy. We did not even impartially examine the facts of the case. Looking back upon that unfortunate misunderstanding to-day, when the old controversies have died away and the old excitement has given place to a newer and larger enthusiasm for the Nationalist Cause, in which Mrs. Besant stands completely united and identified with the Nationalist Party in India,—we are forced to recognise very wide difference between the attitude of the Government and that of Mrs. Besant in this matter. I cannot hold that Mrs. Besant's attitude was at all friendly to our Nationalist Movement in 1905 and 1906 or 1907. But at the same time, neither can it be said that the action which she took towards the Bengalee boys of her school, was altogether unreasonable. The object of the Government officials in Bengal was to stifle the Nationalist agitation. Mrs. Besant's object was to maintain the discipline of the school and college which she controlled. And that is a very vital difference.

Mrs. Besant published an explanation of her policy and action in this matter in the November-number of her Hindu College Magazine. In this explanation she made it perfectly clear that (i) she considered the Curzonian Partition of Bengal, as "a most ill-advised measure ;" (ii) she regarded "the temporary boycott of British goods, *if carried out without intimidation of any kind,* as a legitimate protest against the inconsiderate action of Lord Curzon, and as a constitutional way of drawing the attention of the British people to the wrong inflicted in their name;" and (iii) she did not interfere with anything that the boys might do, to show their love for their country or their indignation against any act or policy of the Government, under instructions from their parents or guardians, outside their school or college; but inside these they must abide by the rules of these institutions, and submit to the orders of their teachers and other authorities of their school or college. In her explanation, referred to above, she said :—

When asked by the Head Master of the Central Hindu College School what it was best to do in the event of the boys coming in mourning; dress to the School, I advised him to give leave of absence to any boy whose father asked for it, but not to allow a political demonstration in the School. When some lads came in undress, and I was asked to explain to them that they could not be admitted, I went to them and asked: "Why do you want to come in mourning ?" "To protest against the Government," was the answer. "No protest against the Government is allowed within College limits," was my reply. "It is the order of our superiors," said a boy. "I know no superiors within these walls," I answered, "excepting the governing body and the teachers. Outside the College, you obey your fathers: inside the College the rules of the place." It will thus be seen that Mrs. Besant's attitude and action in this matter was strictly correct and constitutional. But though it would not be fair to infer from it that she was hostile to the Nationalist Movement in Bengal of the last decade, yet it can scarcely be denied that she was neither positively and actively friendly towards it. I feel confident that if a similar occasion arose to-day, and Mrs. Besant was in charge of any School or College, she will take a similar view of her duty and prevent any political demonstration inside the school or college; but at the same time, having refused admission to the boys to their classes, she would most likely go out with them and organise public protests against bureaucratic repression outside the school or college precints. And that is because of the changed angle of vision through which she sees the Nationalist Movement in India to-day.

Nor is it so very difficult to understand the inner psychology of her previous attitude towards our Nationalist activities in 1905 to 1909 or 1910. In the first place, the educationist and disciplinarian in

Mrs. Besant had thrown the politician in her almost completely into the back-ground in those days. She had ceased to have any political activities or associations ever since she had joined the Theosophical Society and had come to India as a worker in that body. Here in this Theosophical Movement she believed she had at last not only found a haven of rest for her own soul, but also a most mighty instrument for working up the uplift of the human race. To save such a mighty instrument of good was naturally her greatest concern in those days. To keep up her own connection with this society was also recognised as absolutely necessary for her own individual self-realisation and the fulfilment of the great mission of her life, after which she had been groping and striving ever since she was a young woman of twenty-four, when she separated from her husband and broke away from the Christian communion. The founders of the Theosophical Society had, in the supreme interest of self-preservation, scrupulously avoided coming into any sort or suspicion of conflict with the Government in this country. One of them, Col. Olcott was still living and in supreme charge of the policy and activities of the Theosophical Society. Mrs. Besant was under his orders, so to say. That respect for the rules and disciplines of their School or College which Mrs. Besant demanded from the Bengalee hoys, on the Partition-day, required that she herself must also equally respect the rules and traditions of the order or organisation to which she belonged, and submit to its disciplines. And these prevented her from identifying herself in any way with the Nationalist Movement of the last decade.

Apart, however, from these moral reasons, Mrs. Besant had, it seems to me, very strong political reasons also for taking up an attitude of more or less open hostility towards our Swadeshi Movement, ten years ago. She regarded the Boycott Movement, which was really the soul of our Swadeshi activities of that period, as she herself said, as legitimate, if it was carried out under certain conditions. And one of these conditions was that its object must be to draw the attention of the British nation, to the wrong inflicted upon the people of this country, in their name. That was we know, the object of the Bengal Boycott as proposed by some of the older leaders of Bengal. The Boycott Vow sent cut by the Indian Association contained, therefore, the qualifying statement that those who took this vow would observe it "until the Partition was repealed or annulled." But the people at large did not take this view. A large percentage of these printed "Vows" that came back from the mofussil, duly signed and attested by the people, had this qualifying phrase scored through. The general feeling in the country was, "Partition or no Partition, Boycott for ever." And this feeling was extended not merely to the boycott of British goods, but also to every form of voluntary associations with the British Bureaucracy in the country. People demanded that members of the Legislative Councils should resign their places; Municipal Councillors should resign their membership of the Municipal Boards; in short, every form of non-official and optional connection with the Government must be cut off. It was, thus, not a declaration of the boycott of British goods only, but practically a declaration of an open war, carried on by the absolutely lawful and constitutional weapons of Passive Resistance against the Government of Great Britain in India. In pursuance of this policy, there was a very widespread attempt in various parts of Bengal to flout constituted authority and create an absolute *impasse* in the administration of the country.

And at the back of it all there was, unmistakably, the inspiration of the real of Isolated Sovereign Independence for India. And this ideal violently jarred upon the innermost instincts of Mrs. Besant. If she is anything in politics, she is a born Imperialist. The Empire Idea had always a strange fascination for her. "I liked big empires in those days," says Mrs. Besant, speaking of her girlish studies in geography,—"there was a solid satisfaction in putting flown Russia, and seeing what a large part of the map was filled up thereby." And it may also be said, I think, without in any way lowering her in the estimation of my countrymen, that Mrs. Besant has always had the natural pride of the Britisher, in the wonderful world—empire which the British people have built up. True it is that with Mrs. Besant, as it is with all refined spirits, this pride of race is not a flatant, vulgar thing; but it is still there, contributing an element of nobility to her character and a faith, born of the past achievements of her people, in their future progress and prospects. She honestly believes that the future of the world is very largely in the hands of the "Teutonic sub-race." This people, is a sub-race of the great "Fifth Race" of Theosophic terminology, generally called Aryan by ethnologists, which includes us as well. But it is of the puissant European races or nations of whom she speaks, more than of the Indian,—in her vision of the immediate future. In her lecture on "The Christ Triumphant," she says (addressing a London audience) : —

"And then see your own type rising, the great fifth race type, the Aryan, spreading over the whole of the habitable world, divided into its various sub-races, each distinguishable enough when pure, as you can distinguish the Kelt from the Teuton, the Latin from the Scandinavian. See how that race is spreading and growing, how it is dominating and ruling, how colonising and building a mighty Empire. Look onwards for some hundreds of years, and you will see that race rising to its summit, building a mighty World-Empire greater than the past has known, into which shall flow all the power and the glory of the nations, in which shall be incarnate that wondrous group of mighty intellects, that now and again comes out into the world to a race when it reaches its zenith, to be incarnated in the future as in the past in that wondrous triumph of the great Teutonic subrace. See how it holds the West, how it is gripping the East; realise that all the spreading has a purpose, and that behind it stands its Manu, guiding and shaping the mighty Empire which yet shall be. Realise that all wars and all conquests have a purpose, that when a nation invades another, oversweeps it, dominates it for a time, that at that period the nation that is conquered profits as well as the conqueror who learns his lesson. When the Greeks conquered part of India they brought with them their Art, and left deep imprinted on the Art of India the mark of Greece the all-beautiful. When from Central Asia there swept down into India the mighty flood of the Mughals, that developed another form of Art and enriched the country they conquered. All these conquests of East by West and West by East work into the mighty Plan, and spread abroad through the nations the treasures that otherwise would be enclosed within the limits of a single country. Open your eyes to wider horizons; see the mightier, larger Plan; realise that a nation is separated to build up something of value to humanity, and then is spread abroad and scattered that it may carry everywhere that which within its own boundary it made. These wars and conquests, these struggles of nation against nation, of race against race, they all have their place in the Plan; they are guided by the Manu, who knows exactly what is wanted for each, and makes the wondrous mingling, by which humanity grows."

MRS. BESANT AND "SWADESHI"

And it was thus, not merely the educationist and disciplinarian in her, but equally also the imperialist in Mrs. Besant must have therefore been naturally suspicious of the Nationalist Movement in Bengal ten or twelve years ago. There was a revolt of school boys and college young men against the disciplines imposed by their schools and colleges. These so-called disciplines were themselves inspired openly by political motives; and their object was to prevent our young men from actively participating in the work of the new Nationalist Movement in their country. These sought to cripple and kill their natural love and devotion for their Motherland. Such patriotic activities are not considered as criminal in any free country. If they were so considered here, it was due to the very unnatural conflict of vital interests between the people and the Government set over them. All this is true. Mrs. Besant fully recognises all these to-day. But in 1905-6, she was not in intimate touch with our Nationalist activities. She judged these from the outside. The Theosophical leaders of Bengal, and particularly Babu Narendra Nath Sen, who was associated with the declaration of the (Bengal Boycott, more or less, shrank away from the whole movement, as soon as it took up a distinct attitude of defiance to the Executive Government in the country. He was particularly repelled by the strike of the Calcutta students following upon the publication of the Carlyle Circular, prohibiting students from taking any part in the Swadeshi and Boycott agitations, and the subsequent declaration of a National University. That strike was neither organised nor authorised by the political leaders of the Province, whether "Moderate" or "Extremist." But Babu Narendra Nath Sen's attitude towards the new spirit in Bengal, must have considerably influenced Mrs. Besant's views of our Swadeshi Movement of the last decade.

She pleaded, no doubt, for what Lord Minto called, "Honest Swadeshi;" which meant the preference of indigenous products over foreign imports, partly from the desire to keep to the distinctive usages and customs of the country, and partly from economic motives, to help indigenous arts and crafts. Mrs. Besant was for this Swadeshi. But she had no patience with the Bengalee Swadeshi Movement. And she rose up in angry protest against it. In the Central Hindu College Magazine for January 1906, she wrote:—

"So much confusion exists in so many minds just now as to the real meaning and objects of Swadeshi movement, and so many attempts are being made to turn it to a temporary political purpose, that it is the duty of those who have been working in it for many years, and who realise its permanent value, to do their utmost to keep it on its proper lines and to preserve it for its proper purposes. Many agitators, who have hitherto been indifferent to the movement, and who have themselves been foremost in using foreign goods and in despising home-made, are now seeking to capture the movement and to turn it into a political weapon. In order to do this more effectually, they attack and abuse those who have steadily urged its importance to the welfare of India, and make the ludicrous attempt to represent themselves as the promoters of the movement and its previous workers as its enemies. Unfortunately even the Government is to some extent deceived by them, and is inclined to regard the movement as seditious, whereas up to this time it has looked on it favourably. There is the more need for quiet and steady workers for India's welfare not to allow themselves to be driven into a mistaken aloofness, but, in all loyalty and with perfect good-will, to continue the propaganda of Swadeshism, as an economic necessity for Indian prosperity.

"No country can escape severe poverty, if it has but one industry, and that industry, agriculture, and even that agriculture of a too narrow kind. Slowly and steadily India has been losing the arts, crafts and industries, which once enriched her people. Her handicraftsmen, perfected by hundreds of generations, are being starved out, for lack of customers to buy their products. In the desperate attempt to save their dwindling trade, those that remain have copied bad Western models, and have striven to produce cheap and worthless goods to tempt "globe trotters" into buying their wares. The cheapness is but apparent, for the work has become tenth-rate, the artistic good vulgar and ill-finished, and the cloths of little wearing value. A man buys a few cheap cloths every year, instead of a couple that last him for many years, and the prices of the "cheap" cloths added together are larger than the price paid for the good ones. Driven out of their own crafts by lack of customers, the craftsmen have betaken themselves to the due possible industry open to them—agriculture. Already overcrowded, it becomes more overcrowded still. The balance of industries is disturbed, ryot and craftsmen no longer support each other, and when a bad year comes, the impoverished ryot and the artisan turned into cultivators are all engulfed in the yawning abyss of famine.

"For all this," she concluded, "Swadeshism is the remedy, and hence we cannot afford to renounce it because some people are trying to use it for local instead of national, for political instead of economic purposes. Bengal is but a single province, however important, and all the rest of India is not to be left to economic decay because Bengal is temporarily disturbed." In this, however, she sadly misjudged the Bengal movement. Swadeshism in Bengal had a twofold object, one economic and another political; and these two were also really one. For, as Lord Curzon had bluntly declared, administration and exploitation were parts of the same duty in the British Government of India. Political power had been used from the very beginning of British domination in this country, to sacrifice Indian industries to the industrial advancement of the ruling race. What Mrs. Besant called economic Swadeshi could not, therefore, be separated really from political Swadeshi or Boycott. Bengal fully understood this; and therefore, refused to use this Boycott as a mere temporary political weapon. But Mrs. Besant, not being in the mid-currents of that movement, and particularly, owing to her isolation from the general political life and activities of the country, and the sympathy that she received in those days from high official circles, in her propagandist and educational activities, having considerable prejudice against the English-educated Bengalee people, who had been the most denationalised of all the peoples of India, could not possibly take a correct and inside view of the Bengal Swadeshi and Boycott Movement. Added to this was her deep-seated Imperialism, which could not brook the idea of complete National Independence for India, and the evident emphasis of the Nationalist Movement in Bengal was on this Independence—Idea. All these things contributed to the undoubted antagonism with which she viewed that Movement ten or twelve years ago.

MRS. BESANT AND NATIONAL EDUCATION

As in regard to the Bengal Swadeshi movement, so also in the matter of our National movement, Mrs. Besant took up a somewhat unfriendly attitude towards our Nationalist activities of the last decade, and it seems to me that it was due to the same reasons. She was fully sensible of the defects of the existing system of education in the country imparted in the Government schools and colleges. But in those days the chief defect of this education, in Mrs. Besant's eyes, was its denational character. Its most fatal fault was that it was not related to the ancient thoughts and ideals, the time-honoured ideas and traditions, of the people, and it consequently made for the complete Europeanisation of the students who came under its influence. "The needs of India," she wrote in a letter to my respected friend Babu Narendra Nath Dutt, in January 1906, "are, among others, the development of a national spirit, an education founded on Indian ideals, and enriched, not dominated, by the thought and culture of the West." The Central Hindu College at Benares was established for the removal of this need. The National Education Movement in Bengal was inspired by the same ideal. Here also we sought to reconcile the ancient thought and culture of our own country with the requirements of modern European thoughts and acquisitions. These words of Mrs. Besant might well be accepted as the motto of the National Education Council of Bengal. But while the inspiration of Mrs. Besant's National Education Movement, of which her Central Hindu College at Benares was the first fleshly embodiment, came mainly from a recognition of the moral and spiritual needs of the people, the inspiration of our National Education Movement, in 1905-6, came mainly from the political conflict into which we were thrown by the agitation against the Partition of our Province by Lord Curzon. There had already been some attempts in the direction indicated by Mrs. Besant, in Bengal long before the Nationalist upheaval of 1905-06. They were the result of the movement of religious and social reaction that flowed over the country in the eighties of the last century. That reaction sought to revive mediaeval ideals of life and religion and tried to justify existing faiths and institutions by these ideals. There was no conscious desire then, to "enrich" the education of our rising generations, "founded upon Indian ideals, by the thought and culture of the West." In that reaction, there was little appreciation of this thought and culture of the West. With this difference—and it was a very vital difference, no doubt, —we had already in Bengal a few schools that sought to impart a Hindu education to Hindu boys. The Arya Mission Institution of

Calcutta was a typical Institution of this kind that followed very closely, the ideals of Mrs. Besant. But it was still under the control of the Director of Public Instruction and the Calcutta University. So was also Mrs. Besant's Central Hindu College School at Benares. That too was not independent of official control. That institution also was not absolutely free to adopt its own curricula in all matters. All that these institutions could do, all that they actually did, was to add such religious and moral instructions as the authorities thought proper, to the Departmental and University curricula. The National Education Movement in Bengal declared for the complete freedom of the schools and colleges which it proposed to establish, from all this official control. The memorandum of Association of the Bengal National Education Council distinctly declared that its object was to work "independently of, but not in opposition to the Government Educational Department and the existing Universities." But this declaration notwithstanding, it cannot be denied that our National Education Movement was prompted, like our Swadeshi and Bycott Movement, by an unmistakable spirit of defiance to the Government. It was, indeed, impossible to avoid it. The wisdom of the leaders might seek to conceal, but no one could possibly destroy the spirit of antagonism to the Government which the Partition of Bengal and in the matter of education, the notorious Carlyle Circular, had aroused in the community. Above all, it could not be helped that the very inception of our National Education Movement came from the opposition of the Government to our Swadeshi and Anti-Partition agitation. For the success of this new National Education Movement, it was, indeed necessary to organise a boycott of Government schools and colleges and the Calcutta University. Babu Rabindra Nath Tagore (now Sir Rabindra Nath) and Babu Heerendra Nath Dutt took a very prominent part in organising this boycott; and a large number of young men refused to sit for the approaching M.A. degree exami-nations. All these were the necessary preparations far the organisation of a National University in Bengal. But some of the "Moderate" and older leaders coming into the leadership of this movement, when it came to be practically organised, removed somewhat this political spirit from it, and this, among other causes, contributed to make it practically a lifeless and barren thing.

Mrs. Besant also, recognising the spirit of revolt against constituted authorities which really initiated this National Education Movement in Bengal, took up a very strong attitude of hostility towards it. She made a violent attack upon it, in course of one of her addresses to the Theosophical Convention in 1905, which drew a firm private protest from Babu Heerendra Nath Dutt, who, as a member of the Convention, was present at that address. And this protest drew a letter from Mrs. Besant, which was published in the daily press at that time, and subsequently reproduced in the Central Hindu College Magazine, which gave her ideas of National Education in those days. In this letter she wrote that—

"This (National) education on its literary side, should include the teaching of Indian literature as primary, and of foreign literature as secondary; the teaching of Indian history as primary, and of foreign history as secondary; the teaching of Indian philosophy as primary, and of foreign philosophy as secondary. On its scientific side, it should include the science of the west, but should also encourage and teach much of the science, specially in psychology and medicine, of the East; on its technical side it should embrace all the provision for the industrial life of the country-industrial chemistry, agriculture, crafts of every kind, engineering and minerology, etc., etc., on its commercial side, sound training in commercial correspondence, short-hand, type-writing, book-keeping, etc., etc. It should establish professorships and fellowships for the encouragement of Sanskrit and Arabic learning, and should give to these the position held in European Universities by Latin and Greek. It should have its chairs of Theology —Hindu, Mussalman, Parsi, and even Christian, since there are in India a few long established Christian communities.

Universities, she said, based on these ideas, should be established in India. And though she was in favour of denominational colleges, as was seen in the organisation and constitution of her Central Hindu College at Benares, Mrs. Besant would have the Universities "Indian" affiliating all without distinction of religions, and "thus preparing their graduates and undergraduates for the life of the world, in which men of all faiths should co-operate for public ends." In seeking to practically carry out this ideal, "one thing," she said, "must not be forgotten—"A vigorous propaganda to induce parents and guardians to send their boys to the Schools and Colleges recognised by, and affiliated to, the Indian Universities, and to induce Indian Princes, merchants and employers of every kind, to give the preference in employment to the graduates and matriculates of these Indian Universities. No scheme, however perfect, which leaves out of sight provision for the future, can succeed."

Her long experience of British public life particularly her long struggles against organised religious and political bodies, had helped to develop Mrs. Besant's strong practical common sense, which is such an uncommon quality in idealists of the class which she represents. These struggles have lent her the cunning which every organism acquires when it has to fight from hour to hour against unfriendly environments for its very life. Ever since she broke away from the old religion in which she was born and brought up, she had been like a hunted animal. And all these bitter experience came to her help in her work in India. The Theosophical Society as we all know, had been under a political cloud during the early years of its life in this country. That cloud had been largely dispelled by the scrupulous aloofness which the Theosophic leaders maintained from all political agitations in India. But Mrs. Besant came to India with the traditions of her political opinions and associations in England, still fresh in people's mind. The Government was fully aware of these. The officials were keenly alive to these. And it is nothing strange that as soon as her Central Hindu College School commenced to show signs of a vigorous life, and began to receive the support of influential leaders of the Hindu community, it aroused official suspicion. It was then that, to quote Mrs. Besant herself, —"came our quarrel with the Chancellor of the University (Allahabad), Sir Anthony Macdonald, who said we were political and disloyal, using education as a cloak for politics. One or two brave officials were punished for helping us. Rich men shrank away, fearing Government displeasure." But though brave men came to its rescue, Mrs. Besant knew from that experience that if she wanted her school to live and do the work which it had undertaken, it would have to live down this political suspicion. And this consideration naturally led her to systematically court the favour of the Government in the interest of her institution. The Central Hindu College School had secured a permanent footing in the country, partly through official sympathy and largely through the financial support of the Indian Princes and

Chiefs. It would lose both if in any way it lent its support to the Bengalee Movement of the last decade. While, therefore, Bengal was seriously thinking of even boycotting His Royal Highness the Prince of Wales when he came on a visit to India with Her Royal Highness the Princess of Wales, in the winter of 1906, as a mark of its protest against the Partition measure, Mrs. Besant was busily engaged in arranging for a visit from Their Royal Highnesses to her institution. In other ways also, Mrs. Besant was busy then to secure the sympathy and support of the official heirarchy in India on behalf of her educational activities. She went on a visit to the Viceroy at Simla in the summer of 1906, "with the idea of helping Theosophy and the C. H. C. (Central Hindu College) by placing them before the official world, and the visit" as she herself says, "proved in every way satisfactory."

"The Viceroy and Lady Mintokindly promised to visit the C. H. C. when they come to Benares, and the Viceroy expressed his approval of the lines on which the College is carried on, as explained by me; I told him of the religious and moral education given at the College, and of our efforts to make the boys patriotic, public-spirited, brave and self-respecting saying that we taught them to be proud of India, their motherland, and also proud of the great Empire of which India was an integral part. He said that he regarded the encouragement of the sense of nationality as most important, and that with a strong feeling of nationality should go also a feeling of love for and pride in the Empire as a whole."

The motives that led her to cultivate Lord and Lady Minto during the troublesome days of 1906, prompted her to cultivate the local Government also. In 1907 therefore, I find a deputation from the C. H. C, headed by her, waiting upon the Lieutenant-Governor of the U. P., and presenting an address to him. Sir James Latouche in course of his reply to his address said :—

"You have adhered to the aims you set before yourselves at the outset. You then resolved that your work was educational, not political; that the great end of education was to make good men, and that to this end it was necessary that religion should influence life. You combine a secular education of a western type, especially experimental science and technical instruction, with religious training founded on the sacred books of the Hindus and particularly on the great doctrine of the Bhagavad-Gita, of devotion to a personal ever-present and loving God. You desire that the education provided should cost little to the students, but should be complete and flexible, turning out students fit to take their part in every department of the larger life of the world.

With such aims the Government, realising as it does the need and abundant scope which exists for variety of educational effort, has every sympathy, and that sympathy has not been the less real, because it has found unostentatious expression in these ways only in which a desire for it has been formed by you. You have always preferred that the College should be unaided by Government and should be independent, and I have always respected that feeling. But not only I, but also the Commissioner and Collector of Benares have always evinced an active interest in your concerns, and I note with pleasure your appreciation of the support which you have invariably received from Mr. Lewis, who has recently retired from the post of Director of Public Instruction.

Finally, I desire to express my respectful admiration of the courageous position taken by Mrs. Besant, the President of the Trustees, on the question of students taking an active-part in political controversy and agitation. She had the courage to do what she knew to be right, even though the course adopted was unpopular for the moment. An institution guided by this principle cannot fail. It is my earnest wish to see the Central Hindu College continuing to send forth into the world young men capable of taking their place in the vanguard of real progress, men who revere God, respect themselves and love their fellow men. Such men will be true patriots, and loyal citizens. This, as I understand it, is the goal towards which you are striving, and in taking leave of you, I can wish you nothing better than that your endeavours may be crowned with the success that they deserve."

And all this shows the real inwardness of the rather unfriendly attitude that Mrs. Besant took up towards the new National Education Movement in Bengal. She saw that, owing to its ill-concealed political emphasis, our National Education movement was foredoomed to failure. Her inherent imperialist instincts also rebelled against the new patriotism in Bengal which had no appreciation of the Imperial connection.

But though unable to sympathise with our new National Spirit, Mrs. Besant fell in with our scheme of National Education and at once set to work for the organisation of a National University for India. She got up an influentially signed petition to His Imperial Majesty the King-Emperor praying for a Royal Charter for the establishment of the University. The special features of this new University would be (i) the inclusion of religious and moral training as an integral part of its educational scheme; (ii) the placing of Indian philosophy, history, and literature, in the first rank and seeking in these and in the classical languages of India the chief means of culture.—"While western thought will be amply studied, eastern will take the lead, and western knowledge will be used to enrich but not to supplant;"— (iii) the paying of special attention to manual and technical training, to science applied to agriculture and manufactures, and to Indian arts and crafts; so as to revive these now-decaying industries. In all these Mrs. Besant entirely followed the Bengal scheme; only she tried to secure that official sanction and authority for it which the Bengal National Council never tried nor hoped to get. But she was doomed to disappointment. The petition for the Royal Charter, while it received the support of Lord Minto, and was forwarded by him to London, came back from there for consideration and report by the Governor-General in Council. And though Mrs. Besant did not give up her attempts, this practically sealed the fate of the proposed National University for India, the whole question being further complicated later on, by the rival movements of a Hindu and a Moslem University which divided the Nationalist force, and practically killed the chances of the National Indian University, which Mrs. Besant tried to establish.

THE THEOSOPHICAL EDUCATIONAL TRUST

In the course of the last four or five years, however, Mrs. Besant has outgrown the limitations of her earlier ideals of Indian education, and has advanced, it seems to me, to the fullest Nationalist Ideal in this as in many other respect. Her Theosophical Educational Trust, therefore, embodies a completer ideal than was realised by her Central Hindu College. This Trust was incorporated in April 1913, that is a little time before Mrs. Besant was drawn into the leadership of Indian Nationalist politics; and it marks, therefore, it may be said an advanced intermediate stage between the Central Hindu College-ideas and the most recent and advanced ideas of full and complete National Education which she has formulated in the Memorandum and Articles of Association of the proposed "Society For the Promotion of National Education"—published on the very eve of her internment. The Theosophical Educational Trust continues the traditions of the Central Hindu College in almost every direction. Like that of the Hindu College, its main object is to impart an education of which "religious instruction shall be an integral part." But it is worked upon a much broader basis than the Hindu College; because the Trust proposes to establish Schools and Colleges "which shall be open to students of every faith." In this matter, the idea of the Trust is to work, on what may be called federal lines. The freedom and integrity of the different great religions are thus, fully recognised; and "Hindu, Muhammadan and Christian prayers are offered every morning, and one period a week in each class is devoted to religious instruction, which is imparted by members of the respective faiths. The Sanatana Dharma Text Book is used for Hindus, the Koran for Muhammadans, and The Universal Text Book of Religions in general." And the object of the last Text Book evidently is to give a universal outlook to the votaries of different religions. The last annual report of the Cawnpore High School, one of the institutions under the Trust, gives the following account of the practical method of religious instruction followed there, which, I think, is a fair sample of what is done in the other institutions controlled by the Trust, and may well be quoted here:—

"After morning roll-call the whole school assembles for prayers. First the famous Shanti—"Sahanavavatu"—is chanted by all aloud together, then the Hindus (who are most numerous) chant their own prayers to music, a Muhammadan boy chants a prayer of his own religion, and this is followed by a Zoroastrian prayer, the three religions of the boys all being thus represented. Afterwards one of the teachers addresses the boys for ten minutes on a special virtue or some other suitable subject. In class special religions are taught twice a week and universal religion once. Theology takes a minor place, and interest is centred round the lives of Teachers and Leaders and

Saints of the religion. In Hinduism the Ramayana, the Mahabarata and Sanatana Dharma Text Books are used. The boys of each religion have their own religious classes and are taught by teachers belonging to their own faith, but in the case of Universal Religion the boys are all taught together, and thus the teachings they have received separately are synthetised." I cannot say if in the early years of her Theosophic mission among us Mrs. Besant believed, like many other Hindu "revivalists", that we could solve our present-day problems by the revival and re-introduction of the ancient ideals and institutions that had long ages ago been killed by the hand of time. It was, indeed, not very easy in those days to clearly distinguish and differentiate her ideas and ideals from those of the general run of our "revivalists." But there can be little doubt now that she occupies a far more rational position than what had been occupied by the popular revivalists of fifteen or twenty years ago. The most vital problem of modern education in India, as the objects and principles of the Theosophic Trust seem clearly to recognise, —is to find out—how and to what extent, we can realise the highest national ideals of education under modern conditions." And it is gratifying to find that in organising this Theosophical Educational Trust. Mrs. Besant has been fully alive to our present-day actualities. The Trust "is trying to revive all that was best in the old relations between Guru and pupil," for instance, "in a form suited to modern times." Let us see, says Mrs. Besant, how far we can reproduce the old-time conditions in their essentials in modern days.

Of old the Guru and his pupil were (*a*) of one race and *(b)* of one religion. In modern days the inhabitants of India are of different races, of different religions, and it is above all necessary to the prosperity and peace of the country that these races and religions should live together in amity and comradeship; ought this comradeship to begin in the school ? The answer to this question will largely depend on the answer to another question : Can boys of different faiths be well instructed in their own religion and be devoted to it, if they are living with boys of other faiths? If this be possible, then will not the school and college which contains boys and young men of different religions be better Nation-builders than those which are confined to students of one religion ?

And Mrs. Besant's Theosophical Educational Trust seeks to "adapt the ancient ideal to modern conditions" in the matter of race, by drawing the Principals, Professors, Head Masters from different races, choosing the test men, irrespective of caste or religion. Under existing Indian conditions, even foreigners may have to be appointed to some of these posts, but it is essential that only such foreigners must be employed who are sympathetic with Indian culture, who are fond of associating intimately with Indians, who will encourage Patriotism, who are without the antagonism of race, and who will obey an Indian as readily as an Englishman, if the former be in a superior position.

By such close association we create the spirit of love and reverence towards their teachers in our students, and we restore the old atmosphere of affection, respect, and confidence. We eliminate race arrogance on the one side and therefore race rebellion on the other, and the racial difference is forgotten and an atmosphere of mutual trust and good-feeling fills the schools and colleges under the control of the Trust.

We have already seen from the description of the religious teaching given at the Cawnpore High School, quotea in a previous para, how a sense of religious unity is sought to be cultivated amid creedal diversity. "I believe" says Mrs. Besant, "that it is possible to realise in our schools and colleges the Theosophical ideal that all religions are branches of the same tree, and that the best plan would be to have a hostel for the students of each great faith, where the food, dress, and customs of living, suitable to each, would be observed. The school or college would be a common building, and the day would be opened by the common religious service. Thus all lads would be drawn together in the daily school or college work, they would feel that they worshipped one God, and yet remain untouched in their loyalty to their ancestral belief. Lifelong friendships would be formed between youths of different religions, thus softening religious antagonisms in later life." In the Trust schools and colleges, we are told, "they all live in a similar way, with the same ideals and hope, full of Patriotism and desire to serve, and ever mindful of the Motherland."

SOCIETY FOR THE PROMOTION OF NATIONAL EDUCATION

It is almost impossible to think that Mrs. Besant, with her education and long experience in politics, did not see that the ultimate ideal which she was striving to reach through her Central Hindu College was fundamentally opposed to the inner trends of the educational policy of the British Bureaucracy in India. Her aim was to make the youths who received their training in the C. H. C. real Hindus and true patriots. She was aiming at producing a class of educated men who would be proud of their country and their culture, who would pursue the ancient disciplines of Bramhacharya for the development of their physique and the purification of their mind, and would combine the knowledge of the west with the wisdom and refinements of the East, and who would thus be able to work out the salvation of their people. True it is, that she did not think of any future of India which would break up the British connection; but it is equally true that her vision of the future was that of a Free India forming an integral part of the British Empire. This political ideal was latent in the movement of educational reform which she inaugurated in her Central Hindu College and School. This was recognised, naturally enough by so shrewd a man as Lord Macdonald. And, as we know he set his face against it.

Mrs. Besant had not received her lessons in the intricacies of British politics without realising the value of compromise in public life. She knew that to achieve the ends she had in view she would have to carefully avoid all conflicts with the official hierarchy in this country, and follow the line of least resistance. Not only herpolitical experiences, but equally also her biological studies had taught her this lesson. No organism that ignores this lesson can succeed in the struggle for existence which is the universal law of all evolution. It was therefore that Mrs. Besant strove in the early years of her educational activities to always carry the Government of the day with her.

This was, it seems to me, one of the real reasons that led her to take up a decidedly unfriendly attitude towards the Nationalist Movement in Bengal in 1905-7. Another reason was, I think, her want of confidence in the educated Bengalee people. Bengal had then a reputation for frothy sentimentalism and incapacity for any solid practical work, among the peoples of India, Bengal had been the most openly Anglicised of all the Indian provinces. The fundamental elements of Nationalism, as Mrs. Besant understood it then, were believed to be absolutely wanting among the educated Bengalees. There were many people even among the advocates of the Swadeshi and Boycott movement in Bengal who too had very little faith in their own countrymen. These people were, like Mrs. Besant, afraid of rousing any serious official opposition to their activities, whether political or educational. These faithless counsels prevailed even in the Bengal National Education Movement, and thereby took away considerably from the inspiration and idealism which the more intrepid and visionary exponents of the new National Spirit had at first contributed to it. The people were alright. They were ready to go to any length and make any sacrifices for the advancement of the Nationalist Cause. But the leaders, particularly, the older politicians, christened as "Moderates" by the Anglo-Indian press, were not prepared to brave these risks and consistently lead them. They were for following the old game of political bluff, and thus win their immediate objective, namely, the repeal of the Partition. We who were in the mid-currents of the Movement, knew that people at large cared very little for the Partition. The agitation against Partition had revealed new and large possibilities before them. The Boycott had given them a new sense of power which they had never felt before. It had brought the masses and the classes together, and had discovered the wealth of intelligence and patriotism that lay hidden in the general unlettered population of the Province. And all these had quickened a new faith in ourselves. Inspired by this new Self-Consciousness and Self-Confidence, Bengal was ready for the highest sacrifices and the most determined efforts for the realisation of the new Nationalist Ideal. But Mrs. Besant did not know all this. She had no idea of the sudden accession of moral strength to the Bengalee people, through the Swadeshi and Boycott activities of the Anti-Partition agitation. And this want of confidence in us, was another reason that led her to take up that unfriendly attitude towards us in 1905 to 1907. I believe that had she been in Bengal then, and had been in intimate touch with our movement and had thus known its immense potentialities, which she has since come to recognise, she would not have taken up the attitude she did in those years.

For all these reasons Mrs. Besant did not favour the active participation of our students in our Swadeshi propaganda. In the December number of her Central Hindu College Magazine, 1905, she wrote:—

I hold that students should not be permitted to enter the arena of party politics while pursuing their studies. The excitement of party struggles indisposes the lads for steady application, and youth runs into wild excesses where mature men remain staid. Political struggles are for men, not for boys, and the hot blood of youth is not to be utilised by politicians to create public ferment and put pressure upon Governments.

As a general proposition this might be acceptable to all; but special conditions make, in this, as in all other matters, legitimate grounds for deviating from it. These conditions had arisen in Bengal in 1905-6. Mrs. Besant knows it to-day, which she did not understand in her detachment from all political activities in 1905-6, that no Nationalist movement can succeed without the enthusiasm and self-sacrifice of the youthful intellectuals of the nation. The students formed the greatest strength of the movement for political freedom in Russia. It was so in Italy before the Liberation, and during all the struggles with the Austrian power in the early years of Mazzini. Like Young Italy, Young Ireland, under Thomas and Duffy formed the soul of the Nationalist movement in Ireland, about the middle of the last century. So it has, indeed, been all the world over. And it could not be otherwise in this country. There are occasions when studies have to be sacrificed to the more urgent and serious duties affecting the advancement or preservation of the National Life. Mrs. Besant did not feel the urgency of the situation which we were called upon to face in Bengal ten years ago. Or, I feel confident, she would have taken a different view of this question.

In fact, the students were only doing Swadeshi work during their holidays. They were, of course, attending our meetings in their thousands during session time, but except doing occasional picketting duty they did no practical work then. It was only during the holidays that they did excellent work in their villages for the advancement of the Swadeshi and Boycott propaganda. And the organisation of these works gave them a field for self-discipline which they never had in their schools and colleges. The excellent education in the development of character, in habits of order and obedience, and patriotic self-sacrifice which the participation of our youthful students in our political agitations offered, was seen clearly manifest in the organisation and work of the National Volunteers of Calcutta during the Ardhodaya Festival of 1907— work that compelled the anxious admiration of the highest officials in the City and the Province.

And it was just these qualities, these new powers and possibilities, in the youths of the nation that made the Government nervous. Here was a new danger to the Government; for these powers and possibilities, if duly developed, might be applied by political leaders to bring pressure upon the authorities and thus force official policy and control official action. This was the meaning and motive of the Circular promulgated above the signature of the Hon. Mr. Carlyle, then Chief Secretary to the Government of Bengal, prohibiting students of Government and aided institutions from joining political meetings or in any way participating in political agitations. This was shortly followed, in a few months, by what is called Risley Circular, named after Sir Herbert Risley who was then Secretary to the Government of India. And these unreasonable restrictions upon our rising generations in regard to all nationalist works and activities, furnished the real motive for our Movement of National Education.

But Mrs. Besant was then not with us, and stood indeed away from all political activities in the country. She has since thrown herself heart and soul into these Nationalist political activities, and has, therefore, come to realise, under pressure of the actualities of the circumstances in which she finds herself and all her political work, the need and value of the ideals and methods that were followed in Bengal ten years ago. These actualities have forced her to repeat the history of Bengal, and, as an essential element of our present Nationalist Movement, to organise an all-India National Education Society, the Draft Memorandum of Association and Rules of which she was able to publish on the eve, almost, of her internment.

In her introductory article to this Memorandum of Association, she discusses the "objects and Reasons" of this project. "The chief educational want of India," she says here, "is Colleges run on National lines and under national control, Colleges which should make it their one duty to train up pious, honourable, brave, and cultured Indian gentlemen, loyal to their Motherland, to the Crown and to the Empire. To fulfil this duty, it is absolutely necessary that the boys should grow up, through their school and college life, in an atmosphere of pure and passionate Patriotism, full of pride in their country, full of aspiration for her service. The high spirit of the boys must be trained and disciplined but never broken; love and not fear must be the root of their obedience, and trust and not terror must characterise their attitude to their teachers."

"Such a College in each Presidency town and major Province—to be the parent of similar Colleges in the Moffussil—is necessary for the growth and training of the National life. The present generation of lads is splendid material, but is mostly uncared for out of the class-hours and unloved by their teachers in the Government and missionary schools; their budding patriotism is treated as sedition, their self-respect as insubordination, their high spirits as rebellion; their National heroes must be worshipped in secret and the National portraits which should hang in their class-rooms must be hidden away in their boxes. We have to train our boys for freedom, and the very qualities, now repressed, are national assets, to be utilised, not eradicated. We need not fear their high spirits, their daring, their pride, their sensitive dignity; these are the jewels of a free Nation, though dreaded by the authorities over a subject people. Our boys must be as free in India, as English boys are free in England."

In a circular letter to leading gentlemen in the country inviting them to join this National Education Society, Mrs. Besant says : —

"As the Government Educational Service becomes more and more rigid and the deadening Official pressure which crushes out patriotism and the sense of pride in the country, becomes heavier, those who work for India's freedom within the Empire are faced by a grim alternative. Either they must stand aside, and see the youth of the country divided into two groups: one servile and cringing, useless to the country and fit only to be servants of the bureaucracy; the other high-spirited and patriotic but desperate, plunging into anarchical violence. The G. O. No. 559 of the Government of Madras deprives the whole school-and-college-going population of the instruction and advice hitherto given to them in political matters by the lectures of leading politicians, cuts them off entirely from the great men of their own country, to be shaped by foreigners and infuses into their minds doubt and suspicion of their natural leaders.

It is, therefore, necessary to do something to save these unfortunate youths from becoming either slaves or rebels, and the wisest plan seems to be to carry into execution a scheme discussed with friends in the various Provinces for some months past, namely to build up a system of National Education entirely apart from, but not in hostility to, the official system, and to offer as an alternative to the Government and missionary schools, an education which will train Indian students as students in other countries are trained, to look forward to a life honourable to themselves and useful to their country, nourishing in their boyhood and youth a noble ambition to be worthy citizens of a great and powerful Nation.

It will thus be seen that as soon as Mrs. Besant threw herself with characteristic earnestness and energy into our current political activities and came face to face with the stern actualities of our present political condition, she was forced to fall into line with the earlier Nationalist ideals and methods of the once-condemned Bengal School, with this possible difference, that while the Bengalee Nationalism of the last decade laid no emphasis whatever on the Empire-Idea as necessary for the highest self-fulfilment of the Nation-Idea and had no appreciation, therefore, of the value of the Imperial connection, Mrs. Besant has emphasised the Empire-Idea and has full appreciation of the Imperial Connection. The question, however, arises here, why did Mrs. Besant, who had almost religiously kept away from all our political activities for so many years, come to throw herself into the mid-current of our political life? To understand this phase of her evolution, we must pass in review her previous political activities in the land of her birth.

IN THE SERVICE OF FREEDOM

Mrs. Besant has been a servant of the Goddess of Freedom from her early youth. For Freedom's sake she forsook her home and her church when she was barely twenty-five, and threw herself upon the surging waters of London's poverty and work. We in India can scarcely realise what it meant to a young and inexperienced woman of gentle birth and good social position. Home, friends, position, she had sacrificed all for Freedom's sake, and had to seek work like the poorest and most helpless of London's poor. She had a small monthly income, but it was only "sufficient" as she says, "for respectable starvation." And she had to keep not only herself but her little daughter also on this pittance. "With what a great price I had obtained my freedom," she says.

"Home, friends, social position, were the price demanded and paid, and, being free, I wondered what to do with my freedom. I could have had a home with my brother if I would give up my heretical friends and keep quiet, but I had no mind to put my limbs into fetters again, and in my youthful inexperience I determined to find something to do. The difficulty was the "something," and I sent various shilling in agencies, with a quite wonderful unanimity of failures. I tried fancy needlework, offered to "ladies in reduced circumstances," and named 4s. 6d. by some weeks of stitching I experimented with a Birmingham firm, who generously offered every one the opportunity of adding to their incomes, and on sending the small fee demanded, received a pencil-case, with an explanation that I was to sell little articles of that description going as far as cruet-stands, to my friends. I did not feel equal to spring pencil-cases and cruet-stands on my acquaintances, so did not enter on that line of business, and similar failures in numerous efforts made me feel, as so many others have found, that the world-oyster is hard to open.

She became for a time, "head-cook, governess, and nurse," in an English family, and received board and lodging for her little daughter and herself, as payment for her work. She gave up this work after sometime, and arranged to set up house with her mother. But Death soon snatched her only earthly help away before the house had been regularly established and she found herself "all alone."

Very hard days followed. Mrs. Besant then took to literary work, and wrote some pamphlets for Mr. Thomas Scott, a genial and ardent free-thinker, and earned a few guineas which were "very valuable." She had to study hard for this work and spend long days in the British Museum. In those days the little money she had was, she says, enough to buy food for two but not enough to buy food for three—the third being a servant whom she had to keep to look after her little daughter when she was away in town studying for her work. And thus it came about that she "would go out and study all day at the British Museum, so as to 'have my dinner in town,' the said dinner being conspicuous by its absence."

"Recalling those days (Mrs. Besant wrote in her Autobiography) of "hard living," I can now look on them without regret. More, I am glad to have passed through them for they have taught me how to sympathise with those who are struggling as I struggled then, and I never can hear the words fall from pale lips. "I am hungry" without remembering how painful a thing hunger is, and without curing that pain, at least for the moment."

Loss of friends, loss of position in social life, hunger, and privation, all these are some of the prices that Mrs. Besant paid for Freedom's sake. Her socalled "Atheism" was only due to a declaration of the Freedom of her reason and her conscience from the superimposed authority of Church and Scriptures. In her pamphlet "On the Nature and Existence of God," (1874), she had acclaimed Truth for her Mistress. Freedom for her General, Love for her Inspirer, and Man for her Master. Finding it impossible to accept the service of a God in whom she could not believe, she consecrated her youthful life to the service of Man. Finding herself outside what men called the Temple of God, which is, alas, too often only a Temple of man's own conceit and arrogance, Mrs. Besant set herself to build a Temple of Man. It was, however, not the Temple of man as she found him about her, but of Man as he will be in the coming ages, —her Ideal Man, perfect in body and mind. It is the Man, as already quoted in a previous page—who will be—

> In form strong and fair, perfect in physical development as the Hercules of Grecian art, radiant with love, glorious in self-reliant power; with lips bent firm to resist oppression, and melting into soft curves of passion and of pity; with deep farseeing eyes, gazing piercingly into the secrets of the unknown; and resting lovingly on the beauties around him; with hands strong to work in the present; with heart full of hope which the future shall realise; making earth glad with his labour and beautiful with his skill.

This is the man whom Mrs. Besant desired to set up in her Holy Temple. Her ideal Humanity was "the Humanity of the freeman who knows no lord, who brooks no tyranny, who relies on his own strength, who makes his brother's quarrel his proud, true-hearted, loyal, brave."

Reviewing these "Atheistic Ideals" of Mrs. Besant, we almost seem to hear her ringing tones, as she threw down this challenge to the Church and Society about her.—"You have made up your God out of ancient superstitions and survivals; I will build up my God out of brother man. You have set up a God who is the exact prototype of the earthly tyrants as you are or as you obey, a God who is ever ready to punish men for their sins and degradations, but who either has not the will or the power to lift them out of their wretchedness, which is the parent of their transgressions. I will work to make a man who will neither tyrannise over others, nor brook tyranny from others, who will be far more eager to uplift than to punish the weak and the fallen. You have set up a God, who is, for all practical purposes, indifferent to our sins and our sorrows, untouched by our sins, and unaffected by our sorrows. I will make a man who will weep with the weeping, and rejoice with the rejoicing humanity. You have set up a God who punishes one man for the sins of another, who condemns unborn babes to eternal punishment for the transgressions of their "first parents," and who can neither be just nor loving, for were he just he could never have punished one person for the sin of another, and if he were loving he could not condemn any of his creatures to eternal torture in hell. I will help to make a man both truly just and truly loving, a man who will stand up for justice even if the heavens fall, and who will bear his brother's sins and sufferings as his own and deny himself everything to lighten his brother's burden or remove his brother's sins. Your God sits invisible up in your heavens. My man stands before my eyes, toiling and struggling in the society about me. This Society is the Temple wherein I worship my man.

In this Temple will I work with my own hands to set up and sanctify and consecrate the object of my worship and my aspiration."

And it is just here, in her so-called "Atheistic Ideals," that we must look for the inspiration of all her social and political activities. A man of faith, as faith is commonly understood, with his eyes and his hopes fixed, in a heaven far away from this work-a-day world, where every wrong is righted and every good rewarded might be indifferent to present sufferings. He might put up with present bondage in the hope of final liberation. He might even ignore the bondage of flesh, in the conviction or consciousness of the "eternally realised freedom" of the soul, as so many of our own people do, including many a sage and saint as well. But to Mrs. Besant, in her youthful "atheistic" days, the world was the only reality, this life the only thing that really mattered, man as he is, in the flesh, now, at this moment, and here in London or Manchester, was her only concern. She had tasted the joys of Freedom herself. She had bought it at a high price. She had known what its absence means. And she wanted every man and woman to taste, to possess, to enjoy this freedom. It was only natural, therefore, that raising the standard of revolt, in the name of Freedom, first in her religious relations, she went with it, holding it high in her hand into every other relation of life, domestic, social, economic, and political. She raised her protest against every institution and arrangement, that interfered with man's right to think, live, and act, just as he thought best, provided only it did not interfere with the equal right of other men to think, act, and live, just as seem best to them. This is how in early youth, her very "atheistic" idealism and the social philosophy that grew out of it, drew her into politics, in which as she herself says, she held, or was believed to hold, "extreme views." She says however:—

Politics, as such, I cared not for at all, for the necessary compromises of political life were intolerable to me; but whenever they touched on the life of the people they became to me of burning interest. The land question, the incidence of taxation, the cost of Royalty, the obstructive power of the House of Lords—these were the matters to which I put my hand; I was a Home Ruler, too, of course, and a passionate opponent of all injustice to nations weaker than ourselves, so that I found myself always in opposition to the Government of the day. Against our aggressive and oppressive policy in Ireland, in the Transval, in India, in Afghanistan, in Burma, in Egypt, I lifted up my voice in all our great towns, trying to touch the consciences of the people, and to make them feel the immorality of a land-stealing, piratical policy. Against war, against capital punishment, against flogging, demanding national education instead of big guns, public libraries, instead of warships —no wonder I was denounced as an agitator, a fire brand, and that orthodox society turned up at me its most respectable nose.

FIRST LESSONS IN POLITICS

In fact, even before she found her "Atheism," and while still passing through what she calls "the storm of doubt," Mrs. Besant learnt her first lessons in liberal, democratic politics, through the heart-rending experiences of the life of the English poor, which she gathered in course of her parish work, nursing the sick, and trying to brighten the lot of the poor, which in return gave her considerable relief in the midst of the anxiety and mental torment which she was herself passing through owing to her growing unbelief in the dogmas of the Church. "I learned then," she says, "some of the lessons as to the agricultural labour and the land that I was able in after years to teach from the platform."

In one cottage I had found four generations sleeping in one room—the great grandfather and his wife, the unmarried grandmother, the unmarried mother, the little child; three men lodgers completed the tale of eight human beings crowded into that narrow ill-ventilated garret. Other cottages were hovels, through the broken rafts of which poured the rain and wherein rheumatism and ague lived with the human dwellers. How could I do aught but sympathise with any combination that aimed at the raising of these poor?

The Agricultural Labourers' union bad been formed about that time, but it was bitterly opposed by the farmers, and they would give no work to a Union man. The farmers hated the Union because its success meant higher wages for the men and it never struck them, says Mrs. Besant, that they might pay less rent to the absent landlord and higher wages to the men who tilled their fields.

> They had only civil words for the burden that crushed them *(i.e.,* the burden of rent), hard words for the mowers of their harvests and the builders-up of their ricks: they made common cause with their enemies instead of with their friends, and instead, of leaguing themselves together with the labourers as forming the true agricultural interests they leagued themselves with the landlords against the labourers, and so made ruinous fatricidal strife instead of easy victory over the common foe. And seeing all this, I learned some useful lessons and the political education progressed while the theological strife went on within.

Her greatest political inspiration, however, came from Charles Bradlaugh to whom she was gradually drawn by the community of their theological opinions. Charles Bradlaugh, whatever people might think or say of his theological opinions, was about the straightest man that British party politics has ever known. John Stuart Mill, himself another pure politician and man, though a heretic in the opinion of the Christian Church, wrote in his Autobiography with regard to Bradlaugh referring to his first Parliamentary candidature,— as follows :—

> He had the support of the working classes; having heard him speak I know him to be a man of ability, and he had proved that he was the reverse of a demagogue by placing himself in strong opposition to the prevailing opinion of the Democratic party on two such important subjects as Malthusianism and Proportionate Representation. Men of this sort, who while sharing democratic feeling of the working classes judge political questions for themselves, and have the courage to assert their individual convictions against popular opposition, were needed, as it seemed to me in Parliament; and I did not think that Mr. Bradlaugh's anti religious opinions (even though he had been intemperate in the expression of them) ought to exclude him. (Quoted by Mrs. Besant in her Autobiography.)

Mr. Bradlaugh had contested Northampton, as a Radical, first in 1868, and next in February 1874. In September of the same year there was a fresh election, and Mr. Bradlaugh again stood for the seat. Mrs. Besant was present at Northampton, during this campaign, and learned there some of the most valuable lessons in political warfare. As is usual in these Parliamentary elections, the supporters of the rival candidates, indulge in all sorts of abuse and slanders against their opponents, even when the candidates themselves do not use such mean tricks to gain their ends. The violent abuse levelled against Mr. Bradlaugh by the Whigs, and the foul and wicked slanders circulated against him, assailing his private life and family relations, angered almost to madness those who knew and loved him. These brutal attacks on his personal character drove them wild.

Stray fights had taken place during the election over these slanders, and defeated by such foul weapons (for Bradlaugh lost the seat) the people lost control of their passions. As Mr. Bradlaugh was sitting well-nigh exhausted in the hotel, after the declaration of the poll, the landlord rushed in, crying to him to go out and try to stop the people, or there would be murder done at the "Palmerston," Mr. Fowler's headquarters; the crowd was charging the door, and the windows were being broken with showers of stones. Weary as he was, Mr. Bradlaugh sprang to his feet, and swiftly made his way to the rescue of those who had maligned and defeated him. Flinging himself before the doorway, from which the door had just been battered down, he knocked down one or two of the most violent, drove the crowd back, argued and scolded them into quietness, and finally dispersed them. But at nine o'clock he had to leave Northampton to catch the mail steamer for America at Queenstown, and after he had left, word went round that he had gone, and the riot he had quelled broke out afresh. The Riot Act was at last read, the soldiers were called out, stones flew freely, heads and windows were broken, but no very serious harm was done. The "Palmerston." and the printing-office of the *Mercury* the Whig organ, were the principal sufferers; doors and windows disappearing somewhat completely.

Four years later in 1878, "when the Beaconsfield Government was in full swing, with its policy of annexation and aggression. I played my part"—says Mrs. Besant, "with tongue and pen, and my defence of an honest and liberty-loving policy in India against the invasion of Afganistan and other outrages, laid in many an Indian heart a foundation of affection for me, and seem to me now as a preparation for the work among Indians to which much of my time and thought to-day are given." This she wrote in 1893, when she was only a preacher of Theosophy to us, but it seems that though not openly participating in our political work at that time, she was not, at heart, indifferent to it. The same year [1878] she wrote a little book on "England, India and Afganistan."

FOR FREEDOM IN IRELAND

Two years later, the autumn of 1880, "found the so-called liberal Government in full tilt against the Irish leaders," and we find Mrs. Besant working hard to raise English feeling in defence of Irish Freedom, even against attack by one so much honoured as Mr. Gladstone.

> "It was uphill work, for harsh language had been used against England and all things English, but I showed by definite figures—all up and down England—that life and property were far safer in Ireland than in England that Ireland was singularly free from crime save in agrarian disputes, and I argued that these would disappear if the law should step in between the landlord and the tenant, and by stopping the crimes of rack-renting and most brutal eviction, put an end to the horrible retaliations that were born of despair and revenge."

From this time onward, Mrs. Besant continued her labours for the freedom of Ireland—"a land so dear to her heart." Ireland was then "writhing in the cruel grip of the Coercion Act, and an article by her on "Coercion in Ireland and its Results"—exposing the wrongs done under the Act, was reprinted as a pamphlet and had a wide circulation.

> "I pleaded against eviction—7,020 persons had been evicted in the quarter ending in March—for the trial of those imprisoned on suspicion, for indemnity for those who before the Land Act had striven against wrongs the Land Act had been carried to prevent, and I urged that "no chance is given for the healing measures to cure the sore of Irish disaffection until not only are the prisoners in Ireland set at liberty, but until the brave, unfortunate Michael Davitt stands once more a free man on Irish soil."

All this was bearing fruit. The Government reconsidered its policy and sent Lord Frederick Cavendish to Ireland "carrying with him the release of the "suspects," and scarcely had he landed ere the knife of assassination struck him—a foul and cowardly murder of an innocent messenger of peace." "It is not only two men they have killed,"—wrote Mrs. Besant a day or two after these murders—"they have stabbed the new-born friendship between two countries, and have reopened the gulf of hatred that was just beginning to close." The crime succeeded in its object, she says, and hurried the Government to pass a new Coercion Act. But even in the face of the public excitement Mrs. Besant pleaded still, "Force no remedy," despite the hardship of the task."

> "There is excessive difficulty in dealing with the Irish difficulty at the present moment. Tories are howling for revenge on a whole nation as answer to the crime committed by a few; Whigs are swelling the outcry; many Radicals are swept away by the current, and feeling that "something must he done." they endorse the Government action forgetting to ask whether the "something" proposed is the wisest thing. A few stand firm, but they are very few—too few to prevent the new Coercion Bill from passing into law. But few though we be who lift up the voice of protest against the wrong which we are powerless to prevent, we may yet do much to make the new Act of brief duration, by so rousing public opinion as to bring about its early repeal. When the measure is understood by the public half the battle will be won; it is accepted at the moment from faith in the Government; it will be rejected when its true character is grasped. The murders which have given birth to this repressive measure came with a shock upon the country, which was the more terrible from the sudden change from gladness and hope to darkness and despair. The new policy was welcomed so joyfully; the messenger of the new policy was slain ere yet the pen was dry which had signed the orders of mercy and of liberty. Small wonder that cry of horror should be followed by measures of violence; but the murders were the work of a few criminals, while the measure of vengeance strikes the whole of the Irish people. I plead against the panic which confounds political agitation and political reddressal of wrong with crime and its punishment; the Government measure gags every mouth in Ireland, and puts as we shall see, all political effort at the mercy of the Lord Lieutenant, the magistracy, and the police." I then sketched the misery of the peasants in the grip

of the absentee landlords, the turning out of the road-side to die of the mother with newborn babe at her breast, the loss of "all thought of the sanctity of human life when the lives of the dearest are reckoned as less worth than the shillings of overdue rackrental." I analysed the new Act: "When this Act passes, trial by jury, right of public meeting, liberty of press, sanctity of house, will one and all be held at the will of the Lord-Lieutenant, the irresponsible autocrat of Ireland, while liberty of person will lie at the mercy of every constable. Such is England's way of governing Ireland in the year 1882. And this is supposed to be a Bill for the "repression of crime." Bluntly, I put the bald truth: "The plain fact is that the murders have succeeded. They saw in the new policy the reconciliation of England and Ireland; they knew that friendship would follow justice, and that the two countries, for the first time in history, would clasp hands. To prevent this they dug a new gulf, which they hoped the English nation would not span; they sent a river of blood across the road of friendship, and they flung two corpses to bar the newly-opened gate of reconciliation and peace. They have succeeded."

But not only in Ireland, but wherever she saw any serious political wrong or oppression, she placed her pen and tongue at the service of the sufferers. We thus find her taking the lead in a movement, which was set on foot in England in 1885. "to draw attention to the terrible sufferings of the Russian political prisoners," and a Society of the Friends of Russia was established at a meeting held in her house, "to spread accurate and careful information about the present condition of Russia. Bradlaugh, "Stepniak," the author of "Underground Russia," and many others were present." "It is noteworthy," writes Mrs. Besant "that some of the most prominent Russian exiles— such as Kropatkin—think that the Tzar himself is not allowed to know what occurs, and is very largely the victim of the bureaucracy that surround him."

MR. CHARLES BRADLAUGH-FIGHT FOR CONSTITUTIONAL RIGHT

Mrs. Besant received her most valuable political lessons, however, through her close association with Mr. Bradlaugh, in his fight for his seat in the House of Commons. After twelve years of continued work, from 1868, when he first stood for the franchise of Northampton, Mr. Bradlaugh found himself at last returned by a large majority, in 1880. But his success at the poll was not the end, but only the beginning, of his struggle for the recognition of the freedom of the conscience of the individual, in his political life and relations. "Parliament was to meet on April 29th, the swearing-in beginning on the following day, and Mr. Bradlaugh had taken counsel with some other Free-thinking members as to the right of Freethinker to affirm. He held that under the Act 29 and 30 Vict. c. 19, and the Evidence Amendment Acts 1869 and 1870, the right to substitute affirmation for oath was clear; he was willing to take the oath as a necessary form if obligatory, but believing to be optional, he preferred affirmation.' Mr. Bradlaugh presented himself at the Speaker's table, and in a written statement asked permission "to be allowed to make a solemn affirmation or declaration, instead of taking an oath." He claimed this by virtue of the Evidence Amendment Acts, 1869 and 1870, saying—"I have repeatedly, for nine years past, made an affirmation in the highest courts of jurisdiction in this realm. I am ready to make such a declaration or affirmation." But a Select Committee of the House decided against the claim. Mr. Bradlaugh having, publicly, claimed his right, as a Freethinker, to affirm instead of taking an oath where the name of God in whom he does not believe appears, and thus make his position clear of all possible misinterpretation or misunderstanding, next appeared before the House "to take the oath in the form prescribed by the law." But an objection was taken to this, by the representatives of political Toryism and Christian bigotry; and this objection was considered by another Committee of the House, which reported against him. He was, however heard at the Bar of the House, in support of his claim and "made a speech so self-restrained, so noble, so dignified, that the House, in defiance of all its own rules, broke out over and ovor again into applause." I quote the concluding part of the speech, as reproduced in Mrs. Besant's Autobiography, to indicate the political faith and principles of the Man, to whom, more than to any one else, Mrs. Besant owes all her political inspiration and training.

> "I have not yet used— I trust no passion may tempt me into using—any words that would seem to savour of even a desire to enter into conflict with this House. I have always taught, preached,

> and believed the supremacy of Parliament, and it is not because for a moment the judgment of one Chamber of Parliament should be hostile to me that I am going to deny the ideas I have always held; but I submit that one Chamber of Parliament —even its grandest Chamber, as I have always held this to be—had no right to override the law. The law gives me right to sign that roll, to take and subscribe the oath, and take my seat there (with a gesture towards the benches). I admit that the moment I am in the House, without any reason but your good will, you can send me away. That is your right. You have full control over your members. But you cannot send me away until I have been heard in my place, not a suppliant as I am now, but with the rightful audience that each member has always had…I am ready to admit, if you please, for the sake of argument, that every opinion that I hold is wrong and deserves punishment. Let the law punish it. If you say the law cannot, then you admit that you have no right, and I appeal to public opinion against the iniquity of a decision which overrides the law and denies me justice. I beg your pardon, sir, and that of the House too, if in this warmth there seems to lack respect for its dignity. And as I shall have, if your decision be against me, to come to that table when your decision is given, I beg you, before the step is taken in which we may both lose our dignity—mine is not much, but yours is that of the Commons of England—I beg you, before the gauntlet is fatally thrown, I beg you, not in any sort of menace, not in any sort of boast, but as one man against six hundred, to give me that justice which on the other side of this hall the judges would give me, were I pleading there before them."

The House, however, was not moved by this appeal and noted that he should not be allowed to take the oath. Summoned to the table to hear the decision communicated by the Speaker, he answered:—

> I respectfully refuse to obey the order of the House, because that was against the law.

The House next ordered the enforcement of Mr. Bradlaugh's withdrawal. "Once more the order is given, once more the refusal made, and then the Sergeant-at-Arms was bidden to remove him." "Strange was the scene," says Mrs. Besant, "as little Captain Gosset walked up to the member of Herculean proportions, and men wondered how the order would be enforced; but Charles Bradlaugh was not the man to make vulgar brawl, and the light touch on his shoulder was to him the touch of authority he admitted and to which he bowed." So he gravely accompanied his small captor and was lodged in the Clock Tower of the House as prisoner, until the House should further consider what should be done to him.

On the following day a leaflet from Mrs. Besant—"Lawmakers and Law-Breakers"—was published; and after reciting what had happened, it concluded thus :—

> Let the people speak. Gladstone and Bright are for Liberty, and the help denied them within the House must come to them from without. No time must be lost. While we remain idle, a representative of the people is illegally held in prison. Northampton is insulted, and in this great constituency every constituency is threatened. On freedom of election depends our liberty; on freedom of conscience depends our progress. Tory squires and lordlings have defied the people and measured their strength against the masses. Let the masses speak." But there was no need to make appeals, for the outrage itself caused so swiftly a growl of anger that on the very next day the prisoner was set free, and there came protest upon protest against the highhanded action of the House. In Westminster Hall 4,000 people gathered to cheer Mr. Bradlaugh when he came to the House on the day after his liberation. In less than a week 200 meetings had thundered out their protest. Liberal associations, clubs, societies, sent up messages of anger and of demand for justice. In Trafalgar Square there gathered—so said the papers —the largest crowd ever seen there, and on the Thursday following —the meeting was held on Monday — the House of Commons rescinded its resolution, refusing to allow Mr. Bradlaugh to affirm, and admitted him on Friday, July 2nd, to take his seat after affirmation. "At last the bitter struggle is over," I wrote, "and law and right have triumphed. The House of Commons has, by rescinding the resolution passed by Tories and Ultramontanes, re-established its good name in the eyes of the world. The triumph is not one of Free- thought over Christianity, nor is it over the House of Commons; it is the triumph of law, brought about by good men—of all shades of

> opinion, but of one faith in justice—over Tory contempt of law and Ultramontane bigotry. It is the reassertion of civil and religious liberty under the most difficult circumstances, the declaration that the House of Commons is the creation of the people, and not a club of the aristocracy with the right of blackballing in its own hands."

The matter went to the Law Courts and the Law Courts decided against Mr. Bradlaugh. His seat was, therefore, declared vacant. He was, however, re-elected by the same constituency. I will allow Mrs. Besant herself to relate what followed.

> He was introduced to the House as a new member to take his seat by Mr. Labouchere and Mr. Burt, but Sir Stafford Northcote intervened, and after a lengthy debate, which included a speech from Mr. Bradlaugh at the Bar, a majority of thirty-three refused to allow him to take the oath. After a prolonged scene, during which Mr. Bradlaugh declined to withdraw and the House hesitated to use force, the House adjourned and finally the Government promised to bring in an affirmation Bill, and Mr. Bradlaugh promised, with the consent of his constituents, to await the decision of the House on this Bill. Meanwhile, a League for the defence of Constitutional Rights was formed, and the agitation in the country grew: wherever Mr. Bradlaugh went to speak vast crowd awaited him, and he travelled from one end of the country to the other, the people answering his appeal for justice with no uncertain voice. On July 2nd, in consequence of Tory obstruction Mr. Gladstone wrote to Mr. Bradlaugh that the Government were going to drop the Affirmation Bill, and Mr. Bradlaugh thereupon determined to present himself once more in the House, and fixed on August 3rd as the date of such action, so that the Irish Land Bill might get through the House, ere any delay in business was caused by him. The House was then closely guarded with police; the great gates were closed, reserves of police were packed in the law courts, and all through July this state of siege continued. On August 2nd there was a large meeting in Trafalgar Square, at which delegates were present from all parts of England, and from as far north as Edinburgh, and on Wednesday, August 3rd, Mr. Bradlaugh went down to the House. His last words to me were: "The people know you better than

they know any one, save myself; whatever happens, mind whatever happens, let them do no violence I trust to you to keep them quiet." He went to the House entrance with Dr. Aveling, and into the House alone. His daughters and I went together, and with some hundreds of others carrying petitions—ten only with each petition, and the ten rigidly counted and allowed to pass through the gate, sufficiently opened to let one through at a time—reached Westminster Hall, where we waited on the steps leading to the passage of the lobby.

An inspector ordered us off. I gently intimated that we were within our rights. Dramatic order: "Four officers this way." Up they marched and looked at us, and we looked at them. "I think you had better consult Inspector Denning before you use violence," I remarked placidly. They thought they had, and in a few moments up came the inspector, and seeing that we were standing in a place where we had a right to be, and were doing no harm, he rebuked his over-zealous subordinates and they retired and left us in peace. A man of much tact and discretion was Inspector Denning. Indeed, all through this, the House of Commons police behaved admirably well. Even in the attack they were ordered to make on Mr. Bradlaugh, the police used as little violence as they could. It was Mr. Erskine, the Deputy-Sergeant-at-Arms, and his ushers, who showed the brutality; as Dr. Aveling wrote at the time : "The police disliked their work, and as brave men, had a sympathy for a brave man. Their orders they obeyed rigidly. This done, they were kindness itself." Gradually the crowd of petitioners grew and grew; angry murmers were heard, for no news came from the House, and they loved "Charlie," and were mostly north-country men, sturdy and independent. They thought they had a right to go into the lobby, and suddenly, with the impulse that will sway a crowd to a single action, there was a roar, "Petition, petition, justice, justice;" and they surged up the steps, charging at the policemen who held the door. Flashed into my mind my chief's charge, his words, "I trust to you to keep them quiet," and as the police sprang forward to meet the crowd I threw myself between them with all the advantage of the position of the top of the steps, that I had chosen, so that every man in the charging crowd saw me, and as they checked themselves in surprise, I bade them stop for his sake, and keep for him the peace which he had bade us should not be broken. I heard afterwards that as I sprang forward the police laughed—they must have thought me a fool to face the rush of the charging men; but I knew his friends would never trample me down, and as the crowd stopped the laugh died out, and they drew back and left me my own way.

Sullenly the men drew back, mastering themselves with effort, reining in their wrath, still for bis sake. Ah! had I known what was going on inside, would I have kept his trust unbroken ! and, as many a man said to me afterwards in the northern town, "Oh ! if you had let us go we would have carried him into the House up to the Speaker's chair. "We heard a crash inside, and listened, and there was sound of breaking glass and splintering wood, and in a few minutes a messenger came to me: "He is in Palace Yard." And we went thither and saw him standing still and white face set like marble, coat torn, motionless, as though carved in stone, facing the members' door. Now we know the whole shameful story : how as that one man stood alone, on his way to claim his right, alone so that he could do no violence, fourteen men, said the *Central News,* police and ushers, flung themselves upon him, pushed and pulled him down the stairs, smashing in their violence the glass and wood of the passage door; how he struck no blow, but used only his great strength in passive resistance — "Of all I have ever seen, I never saw one man struggle with ten like that," said one of the chiefs, angrily disdainful of the wrong he was forced to do—till they flung him out into the Palace Yard. An eyewitness thus reported the scene in the Press: "The strong, broad, heavy, powerful frame of Mr. Bradlaugh was hard to move, with its every nerve and muscle strained to resist the coercion. Bending and straining against the overpowering numbers, he held every inch with surprising tenacity, and only surrendered it after almost superhuman exertions to retain it. The sight-little of it was seen from the outside—soon became sickening. The overborne man appeared almost at his last gasp. The face, inspite of the warmth of the struggle, had an ominous pallor. The limbs barely sustained him…The Trafalgar Square phrase that this man might be broken but not bent, occurred to minds apprehensive at the present appearance of him."

They fling him out, and swift, short words were there interchanged "I nearly did wrong at the door," he said afterwards, "I was very angry." I said to Inspector Denning, "I shall come again with force enough to overcome it," He said, "When?" I said, "Within a minute if I raise my hand." He stood in Palace Yard, and there outside the gate was a vast sea of heads, the men who had journeyed from all parts of England for love of him and in defence of the great right he represented of a constituency to send to Parliament the man of its choice. Ah! he was never greater than in that moment of outrage and of triumphant wrong; with all the passion of a proud man surging within him, insulted by physical violence, injured by the cruel wrenching of all his muscles — so that for weeks his arms had to be swathed in bandages—he was never greater than when he conquered his own wrath, crushed down his longing for battle, stirred to flame by the bodily struggle, and the bodily injury, and with thousands waiting within sound of his voice, longing to leap to his side, he gave the word to tell them to meet him that evening away from the scene of conflict, and mean-while to disperse quietly, "no riot, no disorder." But how he suffered mentally no words of mine may tell, and none can understand how it wrung his heart who does not know how he reverenced the great Parliament of England, how he honoured law, how he believed in justice being done; it was the breaking down of his national ideals, of his pride in his country of his belief that faith would be kept with a foe by English gentlemen, who with all their faults he thought, held honour and chivalry dear. "No man will sleep in gaol for me tonight," he said to me that day; "no woman can blame me for her husband killed or wounded, but—" A wave of agony swept over his face, and from that fatal day Charles Bradlaugh was never the same man. Some hold their ideals lightly, but his heartstrings were twined round his; some care little for their country—he was an Englishman, law-abiding, liberty-loving, to his heart's core, of the type of the seventeenth-century patriot, holding England's honour dear. It was the treachery that broke his heart; he had gone alone believing in the honour of his foes, ready to submit to expulsion, to imprisonment, and it was the latter that he expected; but he never dreamed that, going alone, amongst his foes, they would use brutal and cowardly violence, and shame every Parliamentary tradition by personal outrage on a duly elected member, outrage more worthy of a slum-pot-house than of the great Commons House, the House of Hampden and of Vane, the House that had guarded its own from Royal violence, and had maintained its privileges in the teeth of kings."

MRS. BESANT AS BOYCOTTER

Mrs. Besant, on her own responsibility, organised a Boycott of all excisable articles after a certain date, if the Government refused to do justice to Mr. Bradlaugh during that period, and to withdraw all their moneys in the Savings Bank, thus seriously crippling the financial resources of the Government. The response from the workers to her appeal to "stop supplies" was great and touching. One man wrote that as he never drank or smoked, he would leave off tea; others that though tobacco was their own luxury, they would forego it; and so on. But she had to reluctantly ask the people to lay aside this formidable weapon, as "we have no right to embarrass the Government financially save when they refuse to do the first duty of a Government to maintain law." The Government having promised to try and remove the wrong on Mr. Bradlaugh and other Freethinkers like himself, the Boycott was not used.

The struggle continued through 1882. On February 7th Mr. Bradlaugh appeared before and pleaded his cause at the Bar of the House for the third time; and closed his speech with an offer that, if accepted, would have closed the contest.

> "I am ready to stand aside say for four or five weeks, without coming to that table if the House within that time, or within such time as its great needs might demand would discuss whether an Affirmation Bill should pass or not. I want to obey the law, and I tell you how I might meet the House still further, if the house will pardon me for seeming to advise it. Hon. members have said that would be a Bradlaugh Relief Bill. Bradlaugh is more proud than you are. Let the Bill pass without applying to elections that have taken place previously, and I will undertake not to claim my seat, and when the Bill has passed I will apply for the Chiltern Hundreds. I have no fear. If I am not fit for my constituents, they shall dismiss me, but you never shall. The grave alone shall make me yield."

But Parliament would do nothing. In three days, February 8th, 9th, and 10th, 1008 petitions bearing 241, 970 signatures were presented to the House, that justice should be done to Mr. Bradlaugh. But the House treated them with indifference. "The House refused to declare his seat vacant, and also refused to allow him to fill it.

Mr. Labouchere brought in an Affirmation Bill, it was blocked. "Out of this position of what the Globe called "quiet omnipotence" the House was shaken by an audacious defiance, for on February 21st, the member it was trying to hold at arm's length took the oath in its startled face, went to his seat, and—waited events. The House then expelled him—and, indeed, it could scarcely do anything else after such defiance —and Mr. Labouchere moved for a new writ, declaring that Northampton was ready, its "candidate was Charles Bradlaugh, expelled this House." Northampton, ever steadfast, returned for the third time—the vote in his favour showing an increase of 359 over the second bye-election-and the triumph was received in all the great towns of England with wild enthusiasm. By the small majority of fifteen in a House of 599 members—and this due to the vacillation of the Government—he was again refused the right to take his seat. But now the whole Liberal Press took up his quarrel; the oath question became a test question for every candidate for Parliament and the Government was warned that it was alienating its best friends."

In May 1882, Mrs. Besant wrote that Charles Bradlaugh was a man—"who by the infliction of a great wrong had become the incarnation of a great principle;" for the agitation in the country grew and grew, until, returned again to Parliament at the General Election, he took the oath and his seat, brought in and carried an oaths Bill, not only giving Members of Parliament the right to affirm, but making Freethinkers competent as jurymen, and relieving witnesses from the insult hitherto put upon those who objected to swearing; he thus ended an unprecedented struggle by a complete victory, weaving his name for ever into the constitutional history of his country."

AGAINST LAWLESSNESS AND CRIMINALISM

I have devoted so many pages to this episode in the training, as I may call it, of Mrs. Besant, because it drove deep into her heart that hatred of violence, and that regard for law and constitutional authority which has been such an abiding feature of all her public activities ever since. Indeed, this regard for law and order, this hatred of all criminal means for the attainment of even justice and right, seem to have been an original element of her mental and moral constitution. The sanctions of law and order, the life-springs of morality, were embedded in the very make and structure of her being. This is why, having repudiated the outer authorities of church and scripture, an outcaste from society, she never fell even by a hair's breadth from the most strict rules of the moral life. And it is very significant that when she was gradually drifting from the Radical politics of Mr. Bradlaugh into Socialism, she was prevented from openly joining this movement for a time—violently repelled by the gospel of lawlessness and physical force which some Socialists openly advocated. Coming across a statement in a Socialist paper, made by a "Social Democrat"—apparently unrebuked by his fellows, that "all means were justifiable to attain" working-class ends, Mrs. Besant strongly condemned it, declaring that those who urged the use of such means were the worst enemies of social progress. She also set herself up against Mr. Hyndman who had prophesied "a bloodier revolution" than that of France, and the extinction of "book-learning" by the coming Democratic upheaval. Speaking of her earlier opposition to the Socialist propaganda Mrs. Besant says, "their uncurbed violence in discussion, their constant interruptions during the speeches of opponents, their reckless inaccuracy in matters of fact, were all bars standing in the way of the thoughtful."

But she took a more charitable view of the Socialists when she name "to know them better." She found that the bulk of their speakers were young men, "overworked and underpaid, who spent their scanty leisure in efforts to learn, to educate themselves, to train themselves, and she learnt to pardon faults which grew out of the bitter sense of injustice and which were due largely to terrible pressure of the current economic and political system, on characters not yet strong enough—how few are strong enough !—to bear grinding injustice without loss of balance and of impartiality. None save those who have worked with them know how much of real nobility, of heroic self-sacrifice, of constant self-denial, of brotherly affection, there is among the Social Democrats."

THE TEACHINGS OF SOCIALISM

But the cry of the poor, poor not through any fault of theirs but through unjust social and economic arrangements, commenced to constantly din into her ears. Having broken away from home and family and all earlier associations, she had found a new haven of love and affection in her new friends and associates in the Free-thought Movement. Her devotion and gratitude to Mr. Bradlaugh were deep and strong. The Socialists were bitterly opposed to this great and powerful Radical. Indeed, the fundamental philosophy of Radicalism was individualistic, and as such radically opposed to that of Socialism which was "collectivistic."

"But the cry of starving children was ever in my ears; the sobs of women poisoned in lead works, exhausted in nail works, driven to prostitution by starvation, made old and haggard by ceaseless work. I saw their misery was the result of an evil system, was inseparable from private ownership of the instruments of wealth-production; that while the worker was himself but an instrument, selling his labour under the law of supply and demand, he must remain helpless in the grip of the employing classes, and that trade combinations could only mean increased warfare —necessary, indeed, for the time as weapons of defence —but meaning war, not brotherly co-operation of all for the good of all. A conflict which was stripped of all covering, a conflict between a personal tie and a call of duty could not last long, and with heavy heart I made up my mind to profess Socialism openly and work for it with all my energy."

In a series of articles in *"Our Corner"* on the "Redistribution of Political Power," on the "Evolution of Society," and on "Modern Socialism," she made her new position clear:—

"Over against those who laud the present state of Society, with its unjustly rich and unjustly poor, with its palaces and its slums, its millionaries and its paupers, be it ours to proclaim that there is a higher ideal in life than that of being first in the race for wealth, most successful in the scramble for gold. Be it ours to declare steadfastly that health, comfort, leisure, culture, plenty for every individual are far more desirable than breathless struggle for existence, furious trampling down of the weak by the strong, huge fortunes accumulated out of the toils of others, to be handed down to those who had done nothing to earn them. Be it ours to maintain that the greatness of a nation depends not on the number of its great proprietors, on the wealth of its great capitalists, or the splendour of its great nobles, but on the absence of poverty among its people, on the education and refinement of its masses, on the universality of enjoyment in life ... Enough for each of work, of leisure, of joy; too little for none, too much for none —such is the Social ideal. Better to strive after it worthily and fail, than to die without striving for it at all."

In course of these articles she urged for the "union of workers against the idlers," saying that "the weakness of the people has ever been in their divisions, in the readiness of each section to turn its weapons against other sections instead of against the common foe. All privileged classes, when they are attacked, sink their differences and present a serried front to their assailants; the people alone fight with each other, while the battle between themselves and the privileged is raging."

One of her articles, describing some Edinburgh slums, closed with the following :—

"Passing out of the slums into the streets of the town, only a few steps separating the horror and the beauty, I felt, with a vividness more intense than ever, the fearful contrasts between the lots of men and with more pressing urgency the question seemed to ring in my ears, "Is there no remedy ? Must there always be rich and poor?" Some say that it must he so; that the palace and the slum will for ever exist as the light and the shadow. Not so do I believe. I believe that the poverty is the result of ignorance and of bad social arrangements, and that therefore it may be eradicated by knowledge and by social change. I admit that for many of these adult dwellers in the slums there is no hope. Poor victims of a civilisation that hides its brutality beneath a veneer of culture and of grace, for them individually there is, alas! no salvation. But for their children, yes ! Healthy surroundings, good food, mental and physical training, plenty of play, and carefully chosen work—these might save the young and prepare them for happy life. But they are being left to grow up as their parents were, and even when a few hours of school are given, the home half-neutralises what the education effects. The scanty aid given is generally begrudged, the education is to be but elementary, as little as possible is doled out. Yet these children have each one of them hopes and fears, possibilities of virtue and crime, a life to be made or marred. We shower money on generals and on nobles, we keep high-born paupers living on the national charity we squander wealth with both hands on army and navy, on churches and palaces; but we grudge every half penny that increases the education rate and how I down every proposal to build decent houses for the poor. We cover our heartlessness and indifference with fine phrases about sapping the independence of the poor and destroying their self respect. With loathsome hypocrisy we repair a prince's palace for him, and let him leave in it rent free, without one word about the degradation involved in his thus living upon charity; while we refuse to "pauperise" the toiler by erecting decent buildings in which he may live—not rent-free like the prince, but only paying a rent which shall cover the cost of erection and maintenance, instead of one which gives a yearly profit to a speculator. And so, year after year, the misery grows, and every great city has on its womb a cancer, sapping its vitality, poisoning its life-blood. Every great city is breeding in its slums a race which is reverting through the savage to the brute—a brute more dangerous in that degraded humanity has possibilities of evil in it beyond the reach of the mere wild beast. If not for Love's sake, then for fear; if not for justice or for human pity then for sheer desire of self-preservation; I appeal to the wise and to the wealthy to set their hands to the cure of social evil, ere stolidity gives place to passion and dull patience vanishes before fury, and they "learn at last, in some wild hour, how much the wretched dare." But her Socialist activities were not allowed to proceed along calm, peaceful, constitutional ways. And, as happens always in these cases, the outrage against law and peace came from the authorities themselves. "The year 1886 was a terrible one for labour everywhere reductions of wages, everywhere increase in the number of the unemployed," all owing to the slackness of trade. A spirit of sullen discontent was spreading everywhere, discontent that was wholly justified by facts."

> "But ah ! how patient they were for the most part, who sadly, pathetically patient, this crucified Christ, Humanity; wrongs that would set my heart and my tongue afire would be accepted as a matter of course. O blind and mighty people, how my heart went out to you; trampled on, abused, derided, asking so little and needing so much; so loving and so loyal to those who offered you but their poor services and helpless love. Deeper and deeper into my innermost nature are the growing desire to succour, to suffer for, to save. I had long given up my social reputation, I now gave up with ever-increasing surrender ease, comfort, time; the passion of pity grew stronger and stronger, fed by each new sacrifice, and each sacrifice led me nearer and nearer to the threshold of that gateway beyond which stretched a path of renunciation I had never dreamt of, which those might tread who were ready wholly to strip off self for Man's sake, who for Love's sake would surrender Love's return from those they served, and would go out into the darkness for themselves that they might, with their own souls as fuel, feed the Light of the World."

But the people could not suffer long in silence. "The unemployed began walking in procession through the streets, and harshness on the part of the police led to some rioting. Sir Charles Warren (the Metropolitan Commissioner of Police) thought it his duty to dragoon London meetings after the fashion of continental prefects, with the inevitable result that an ill-feeling grew up between the people and the police." A Socialist Defence Association was then formed "to help poor workmen brought up and sentenced on police evidence only, without any chance being given them of proper legal defence." Mrs. Besant organised a band of well-to-do men and women who promised to obey a telegraphic summons, night or day, and to bail out any prisoner "arrested for exercising the ancient right of walking in profession and speaking." But the Police interfered not only with the unemployed processions. They sought to prevent even a meeting of the Metropolitan Radical Federation, which was called to protest against the imprisonment of Mr. O' Brien, the Irish patriot, and as Mr. Matthews, (the then Home Secretary, I think,) had stated from his place in the House of Commons, that there wag no intention of interfering with *bona fide* political meetings the Radical clubs did not expect police interference. But all the same this interference did come. The Police Commissioner issued orders forbidding all meetings in Trafalgar Square; and procession within a certain area. But the organisers decided to go to the Square as arranged, and, if challenged by the police, to protest formally against the illegal interference, then break up the processions and leave the members to find their own way to the Square. It was also decided to go Sunday after Sunday to the Square, until the right of public meetings was vindicated.

According to this arrangement Mrs. Besant, as one of the speakers, was in one of the processions. And what happened had best been described in her own words : —

> As we were moving slowly and quietly along one of the narrow streets debouching on Trafalgar Square, wondering whether we should be challenged, there was a sudden charge, and without a word the police were upon us with uplifted truncheons; the banner was struck down, and men and women were falling under a hail of blows. There was no attempt at resistance, the people were too much astounded at the unprepared attack. They scattered, leaving some of their number on the ground too much injured to move, and then made their way in twos and threes to the Square. It was garrisoned by police, drawn up in serried rows, that could only have been broken by a deliberate charge. Our orders were to attempt no violence, and we attempted none. Mr. Cunninghame Graham and Mr. John Burns, arm-in-arm, tried to pass through the police, and were savagely cut about the head and arrested. Then ensued a scene to be remembered; the horse police charged in squadrons at a hand-gallop, rolling men and women over like ninepins, while the foot police struck recklessly with their truncheons, cutting a road through the crowd that closed immediately behind them. I got on a waggonette and tried to persuade the driver to pull his trap across one of the roads, and to get others in line, so as to break the charges of the mounted police; but he was afraid, and drove away to the Embankment, so I jumped out and went back to the Square. At last a rattle of cavalry, and up came the Life Guards cleverly handled but hurting none, trotting their horses gently and shouldering the crowd apart; and then the

Scott's Guards with bayonets fixed marched through and occupied the north of the Square. Then the people retreated as we passed round the word, "Go home, go home." The soldiers were ready to fire the people unarmed; it would have been but a massacre. Slowly the Square emptied and all was still. All other processions were treated as ours had been and the injuries inflicted were terrible. Peaceable, law-abiding workmen, who had never dreamed of rioting, were left with broken legs' broken arms, wounds of every description. One man, Linnel, died almost immediately, others from the effects of their injuries. The next day a regular Court-martial in Bow Street Police Court, witnesses kept out by the police, men dazed with their wounds, decent workmen of unblemished character who had never been charged in a police court before, sentenced to imprisonment without chance of defence. But a gallant band rallied to the rescue. William T. Stead, most chivalrous of journalists, opened a Defence Fund, and money rained in; my pledged bail came by the dozen, and we got the men out on appeal. By sheer audacity I got into the police-court, addressed the magistrate, too astounded by my profound courtesy and calm assurance to remember that I had no right there, and then produced bail after bail of the most undeniable character and respectability, which no magistrate could refuse. Breathing-time gained a barrister, Mr. W. M. Thompson, worked day after day with hearty devotion and took up the legal defence. Fines we paid, and here Mrs. Marx Aveling did eager service. A pretty regiment I led out of Milbank prison, after paying their fines; bruised, clothes torn, hatless, we must have looked a dis-ruputable lot. We stopped and bought hats, to throw an air of respectability over our *cortege,* and we kept together until I saw the men into train and omnibus, lest, with the bitter feelings now roused, conflict should again arise."

The indignation against the Executive, "grew and grew; the police were silently boycotted, but the people were so persistent and so tactful that no excuse for violence was given, until the strain on the police force began to tell, and the Tory Government felt that London was being hopelessly alienated; so at last Sir Charles Warren fell, and a wiser hand was put at the helm."

MRS. BESANT'S POLITICAL PRINCIPLES AND METHODS

Mrs. Besant came to us with all these experiences of political work in England. She brought with her the great lessons that these had taught her. Her ideals did not demand sexless acquiscence to social or political wrongs. No tyranny must be brooked. No wrong must be permitted to continue. It must be resisted. To resist, wrong is a primary civic duty as much as to assit the right and work for its establishment. But the resistance must be lawful. The method must be constitutional. Evil laws must be replaced by good laws; but there must not be any disregard of Law itself. This Law, as she understood it, is the Expression of the Will of the People. It is the Expression of the Will of the majority. This Will of the People finds expression, in the United Kingdom, through the will of the Parliament. The Will of the Parliament must, therefore, be obeyed. But the Executive orders that are passed, under the discretionary powers given by Parliament to its executive officers, have not the same authority as the positive laws of the land. These orders, if considered to be unjust or harmful to the public well-being, may be disobeyed. But this disobedience should be lawful and constitutional, and should, on no account, take the form of physical resistance. Above the will of the Parliament stands the will of those whom the Parliament represents. The members of Parliament come and go, they are fleeting, impermanent; but the People live for ever. The will of the constituency which a member represents, must command his allegiance first. But above all outer authorities, stands the individual's own Reason and Conscience. In case of conflict between his own Reason and Conscience on the one side, and the collective will of the community to which he belongs, on the other, the individual must accept the authority of the former. But in this conflict, his duty is limited to the assertion of his personal right, within the limits of his individual life and relations only, but he cannot force it upon other individuals or upon society at large. Here he can only refuse to do that against which his conscience or reason revolts; but he cannot break up the social authority by force. Here, while refusing to obey or accept a wrong, he has to willingly take the consequences of his disobedience, as ordained by the will and ordinance of his society. This is, briefly, the principle of Passive Resistance. This Passive Resistance may be individual or even collective and organised. It is permissible in all ethics and civilised polity. It is perfectly constitutional. Mr. Bradlaugh used this weapon in his fight against Parliament, for his right to sit in the House. He disobeyed the wrong order of the House, but offered no resistance when the House punished him for his disobedience. When the House committed him to the Clock Tower, he did not resist that order. "When the authorities of the House refused him admission, he declined to obey them, but asserted his legal right in a legal way, but did not bring in his following to physically force himself into the House. When the Metropolitan Police Commissioner prohibited public meetings and processions, his order was a mere executive order. He passed it in the exercise of his discretionary powers. He did it, in spite of the assurance of his superior officer, the Home Secretary, that *bona fide* political meetings or processions would not be interfered with. People were under no obligation to obey it. So they disobeyed the order. But did it peacefully and constitutionally. They were assaulted brutally, but did not return blow for blow. They resisted violence by suffering. These are the principles that Mrs. Besant had learnt from her political activities and experience in England. These are the methods that she had followed there. Obedience to Law and Respect for the Constitution— these are writ large upon all her political activities and agitations in her home-land. Wrong laws must be changed, but always by lawful agencies. Imperfect constitutions must be amended and led to reach to greater and greater perfection, but always by strictly constitutional methods. Mrs. Besant has not swerved by even a hair's breadth from these principles in all her life.

But she not only brought these fundamental principles of political agitation with her to this country, but she also brought her great and lofty Imperialism with her, when she came to this country. These were the bed-rock of her political philosophy, even when she religiously kept aloof from all political activities among us, and confined herself absolutely to the Theosophic propaganda. And it is these that explains her earlier as well as her latest attitude towards the new Nationalist Movement in this country.

BENGAL NATIONALISM AND MRS. BESANT

This Movement was first born in Bengal. It was more than a mere political Movement. The Political Nationalism of Bengal of the last decade was only a *phase* of a much larger movement of Freedom which dates from Raja Ram Mohan Roy. Its first outer and organised manifestation was in the individualistic revolt of the Brahmo Samaj under Maharshi Debendra Nath Tagore and Brahmananda Keshub Chundra Sen. The next phase in its evolution was seen in the Hindu Revival Movement that followed, as a protest against the undue domination of alien ideas and ideals, which had marked, to some extent, the Brahmo Samaj. It was the beginning of the " Return of the National Self in India to Itself" —as the Hegelians would say. Both the earlier outer and protest movement and the later movement of return and reaction, were moved, one consciously and the other unconscioualy, by the modern spirit of personal and National Freedom. Through both Bengal received her training for that larger and fuller movement of Nationalism which she made vocal in the last decade.

Mrs. Besant's first difficulty in correctly appraising our new Nationalism was the domination of Bengal. When she first came to us, the most dominant thought-force in Bengal was that of the Brahmo Samaj. The Brahmo Samaj was still emphasising the revolt of individual reason and conscience. It represented, underneath all the theological differences between itself and the Freethought movement of Mrs. Besant's youthful days, the spirit of the individualistic freedom of that movement. Mrs. Besant had discovered the limitations of it. She had overgrown that spirit of revolt. In the first flush of her Theosophic initiation, she had been dazed and dazzled by the new Light and Peace which she had found in the Theosophic Gospel. She had not yet recovered her full equilibrium. No novice or initiate finds it. It would, indeed, be fatal to that enthusiasm and devotion which are essential for the education of the novice, and his gradual elevation to these heights, to the lowest rung of which he has just been raised. The process of the initiation is essentially hypnotic. The Master, through his own power, gives the novice and the initiated, a direct foretaste of the highest peace and perfection. In the onrush of this new experience, the novice forgets the value of his past experiences, thinks all previous efforts as wasted, cannot imagine that those errors and falsehoods, those faults and fancies, were necessary links in the evolutionary process that has ultimately brought him to the Master's Feet. He revolts as strongly against his own earlier doubts and denials, as he had done against previous faiths and institutions. Mrs. Besant was in this stage, when she first came to us, intoxicated with the new wine of Theosophy. She found in the Brahmo Samaj the most powerful protagonist of her Theosophical propaganda. It was only natural, therefore, that she would have no love or regard for this movement. She had no appreciation then, even of the Gospel of Freedom which the Brahmo Samaj had preached, and the exceedingly valuable and essential spade-work that it had done, for that Reconciliation and Synthesis for which the Theosophical Society was striving. And Mrs. Besant's unfriendly attitude towards the Brahmo Samaj largely influenced the view that she took of our new Nationalist Movement ten years ago.

For to her, the majority of English-educated Bengalees had the taint of the denational spirit of the Brahmo Samaj. When Bengal started the Swadeshi Movement Mrs. Besant was repelled by what seemed to her to be the inherent hypocrisy of it. "Many agitators" she wrote in January 1906, evidently referring to the Bengalee Nationalists—"who have hitherto been indifferent to the movement, and who have been foremost in using foreign goods and despising homemade, are now seeking to capture the movement and to turn it into a political weapon." Bengal, she said, had been the greatest sinner against Swadeshi, and it did not lie in her mouth to abuse others, who though true and honest Swadeshists, did not approve of the political Swadeshi of the Bengalee people. On another occasion she raised her protest against considering the cry of "Bande Mataram"—which was a salutation to the Mother, as a "Bengal Cry." In this, and other ways, Mrs. Besant showed, in 1905—1906 and the years that followed, her want of regard and appreciation of the Bengalee people.

And this, seems to my mind, to have in fluenced her estimate of, and her attitude to, our Nationalists Movement of the last decade.

But there were other and more fundamental reasons of it also. And one of the most prominent of these, I think, was the undoubted emphasis of that Movement upon the idea or ideal of isolated sovereign independence, which necessarily involved the break-up of India's connection with the Empire. Some of the leaders of the new Nationalists thought might not have this separatist ideal in view, and might have had a broad and truly Imperialist view of the political future of India, but the masses undoubtedly were fired by the ideal of complete national independence. Time was not yet ripe also, for the preaching of the larger Federal or Imperial ideal to the people. The most urgent need then was to quicken the self-consciousness of the nation. And the first stage of the realisation of the self, whether of individuals or nations, is universally marked by a conceit of isolation from, and conflict with the not self. The first step in the cultivation of self-consciousness is to repudiate the identity of the self with whatever stands outside itself. "Neti" "Neti"— not this, not this,—which means the negation of all outer relations of the self, — this is the old, old formula of our Vedantic self-relation, in the first stage of *sadhana.* The new Nationalist thought-leaders followed this formula in their attempts to awaken the self-consciousness of their people. This is the real reason why the emphasis of all their teachings in those days was more upon the ideal of isolated sovereign independence than upon what may be best described as Federal Autonomy.

Nor can it be honestly denied that these new leaders did deliberately provoke an open conflict with the Government. For they saw that unless this was done, they could not kill the fear and inertia that possessed the masses. They did not overstep the limits of law, it is true; but they declared a campaign of Passive Resistance, which it was very easy for Bureaucratic repression to drive beyond the limits of the positive laws of the land. The Anglo-Indian papers, and some of our own papers, and notably the *Indian Mirror,* owned and edited by Babu Narendra Nath Sen, who was a very prominent member of the Theosophical Society and whose views naturally had very great influence in Theosophic circles, also took up a distinct hostile attitude to this new National spirit, and interpreted it as essentially revolutionary. Babu Narendra Nath had proposed the Boycott Resolution of the first all-Bengal demonstration in the Calcutta Town Hall against the proposed Partition of the Province. The authors of that Resolution took up the position which Mrs. Besant considered justified, namely, as a protest against an unpopular public measure and as a means of drawing the attention of the British people to the outrage which their representatives were committing upon the cherished sentiments of the Bengalee people. The Nationalist School, however, took a different view of it. They did not like the habit of always looking to the British people for the redress of Indian grievances. They were not inclined to differentiate between the British Bureaucracy here and the British Democracy in Great Britain. They recognised the fundamental conflicts of political and economic interests between India and Great Britain, under the existing political relations between them. They proclaimed that politics was universally a game of national self-aggrandisement; and the biological law of struggle for existence, as popularly interpreted, which is a struggle between rival organisms for the appropriation of the most efficient means of self-preservation and self-propagation, had its counter-part in politics; where the struggle was between rival nations or states for the appropriation of the largest and the best means of national subsistence and national advancement—a struggle in which no nation ever feels any scruple to crush other nations, if it suits its national ends. There was, therefore, no room for generosity in political life and relations, any more than there is in biological relations, or evolutions. Nations become generous when generosity seems to pay, and when it is calculated to serve their own national ends, and not merely those of any other nations. Individuals may sacrifice themselves for the good of their community or for the advancement of humanity, but nations never can or do so, in the present stage of our social evolution, and sacrifice their interests to promote those of other nations. Individual self-sacrifice is inspired by considerations of the good of their community, which is larger than the individual. But nations have not as yet become conscious of anything higher than nationality, not in any case in Europe. The concept Humanity is, no doubt, larger and higher than the concept Nationality. But this Humanity is as yet practically a mere abstraction in European life and thought. In any case, this Humanity has hardly any room for the non-white peoples of the earth, as organic elements of it. Practically what the Europeans call Humanity, is not really Humanity, but only Whitemanity. And even the organic unity of these White races has not as yet been fully grasped by European political thought. There may, therefore, be international "compromises," but really no international sacrifices for the common ends even of this Whitemanity. Europe has not as yet discovered, therefore, any high ground of Internationalism which might reasonably reconcile the conflicts and competitions of national life. And as long as Europe has not found out this higher synthesis, international relations must inevitably lead to conflicts and competitions of national interests, and the gain of one nation must spell the proportionate loss of another nation. The new Nationalist thought in India clearly recognised all these actualities of the present British Rule, and therefore, sought to awaken a due sense of this inevitable conflict of political and economic interests between India and Great Britain.

We do not regret having done this. Without this conflict, the issues between India and Great Britain could not be made clear and definite. And unless this was done, there could not possibly be any rational ground or basis for working out a full and final reconciliation between them. The excessive and what may be characterised even as unreasonable and shortsighted,—emphasis on National Rights and Interests, as not only considered apart from, but even positively opposed to, Imperial Rights and Interests, was, therefore absolutely needed to prepare the ground for that complete reconciliation between Indian Nationalism and British Imperialism, upon which the perpetuation of the British connection absolutely depends. But for that emphasis and the conflicts that it led to, the present Imperialist Ideal as the objective of India's National political evolution, would never have so fully dawned upon the consciousness of the Indian politician or statesmen; nor would the need of reasonable and timely compromise between the legitimate demands of Indian Nationalism and the reasonable requirements of British Imperialism, have been brought home to the British politicians and administrators to-day.

But Mrs. Besant not being *in* the movement, could not seize the inwardness of it. All that she recognised in it was a revolt against the British Connection, a desire to break up the unity of the great and world-wide Empire that Great Britain had built up. She knew that the actualities of this Empire fell far short of her ideal of Imperial Union. To her, the Empire, was a larger instrument and symbol of the evolving universal brotherhood of Man, which it was the dream of Theosophy to realise on earth. She had learnt the great lesson of history, that tribes meeting to fight one another, end by uniting to form larger social units, thus enlarging the range of human brotherhood from narrower to broader limits. Nations too coalesce with one another, through wars and conquests, to form larger social and political units. In history all conflicts find their final end and justification in a closer unity of the fighting races or nations. This eternal purpose of history was present even in the modern historic evolution of India. Great Britain was advancing it in India, even through the temporary subjugation of the multitudinous races of this country, to her rule. If Great Britain was helping to unite and modernise India, India too was helping to liberalise and spiritualise Great Britain. The two were mutually helping each other to higher planes of thoughts and ideals, and advancing the general cause of universal human fellowship and progress at the same time. The break-up of the connection between India and Great Britain, would not only be ruinous to both these countries, but would be harmful to universal human progress. This is, I think, how Mrs. Besant must have felt in the earlier years of our present Nationalist Movement.

There was, perhaps, another, and more practical, ground of her lack of sympathy with that Movement in 19056 and '07. She had, then, no confidence in the Bengalee people. They had never, within living memory, given proof of any sustained strength or any capacity for united and organised political work. "The danger of popular movements in India" said Mrs. Besant in the course of an address to the C. H. C. students, in 1907, was "rival leaders, quarrels, opposing parties." In another address, she declared, — "A band of patriots is not a mob, blown hither and thither, but a body of men moving towards a common end, and that is wanted in India more than anything else. There is here no cohesion, because there is no discipline, no training in the following of a chosen leader, and the subordination of an individual's wish." And here also, it seems to me, she may have had Bengal before her eyes, more than any other Indian province. For, the Nationalist Movement in Bengal had led to all sorts of divisions, rivalries, and mutual recriminations. She had read of these in the papers. Our crowded meetings swayed by a great and towering passion, were often times described as unruly mobs by our enemies. And all these must have prejudiced Mrs. Besant against our Movement in those days. Not being in it, she could not see how beneath all these outer froth and disorder, there was growing up a new Bengalee, ready to labour and to dare for the sake of his Motherland; a Bengalee, who was disciplined, not by the laws and regulations of outer organisations, but by the impulses of his own soul, to work under and obey, without question, those whom he elected or accepted into the leadership of the new life of his nation. She did not know that large numbers of our young men had been taught, as if by unseen hands, the lesson of self-discipline and self-sacrifice, and how the elders had "learnt to rule and the youngers to obey." "This" is, what she says, makes the strength of a nation. She did not know that this strength has come to us.

And when she could no longer deny that a mighty change had come over the young men of Bengal, and that they had learnt, how and from whom no one knew,—the supreme lessons of discipline and self-sacrifice, and could form mighty organisations, almost out of nothing and from nowhere,— her inherent love of law and constitution, rose up in arms against the acts of violence and wanton murder with which the new and unexpected developments of Bengalee character came to be associated in certain quarters. In this propaganda of political criminalism, she recognised a very serious danger to the future both of India and the Empire. Like many other people, she attributed this revolutionary outbreak to the notorious aping habits of the educated Bengalee. She thought that they were playing at revolutions, seeking for stage effect, by imitating the methods of the European anarchists of whom they had read in books. However she may have been repelled by it, she did not, therefore, take the new revolutionary developments in Bengal, very seriously. Like many others, she thought it was more or less of a mere school-boy affair, which would soon spend itself, or which, otherwise, could be completely suppressed by a little vigorous treatment. This is why, it seems to me, she not only did not raise her voice against the repressive policy of Lord Minto, but even silently lent her support to it. Another reason of it, might possibly be, her personal relations with the Viceroy and particularly with the Vicereine, who was really the power behind the throne, in those days in India, and the unshaken faith that she had in their sincere desire to do good to India.

To sum up, then, Mrs. Besant set herself up against our new Nationalist Movement of the last decade, for three reasons, (i) her want of faith in the Bengalee character, (ii) her inherent Imperialism, (iii) her strong antipathy towards all lawless and unconstitutional methods and physical violence in the pursuit of political rights. To these may be added a fourth, of a more personal nature, namely, her close and intimate relations with Lord and Lady Minto, which revealed to her their sincere love and goodwill for the Indian people.

FROM OPPOSITION TO LEADERSHIP

It was not long, however, before Mrs. Besant realised that the revolutionary movement, whatever might be its actual strength or extent, had taken a deeper root than was at first supposed. Repression had been tried, and had failed. Partial conciliation also had been tried, and that too had failed to touch even the outermost fringe of that unrest, out of which this revolutionary spirit had grown. Something more was needed to cure it. The days of petty concessions were gone. Something must be done that would, in the words of His Highness the Maharaja Saheb of Bikaneer, "appeal to the imagination of the people," and offer permanent reconciliation between the legitimate demands of Indian Nationalism and the reasonable requirements of the unity and integrity of the British Empire. She saw that this reconciliation could come only through the establishment of Home Rule in India. With this cry of Home Rule she came, therefore, to us in 1913, from her last visit to England; and was at once openly welcomed by every thought-leader in the new Nationalist Movement, into the leadership of it.

MRS. BESANT AND THE HOME RULE MOVEMENT IN INDIA

And one is forced to recognise the statesmanship of this great and life-long fighter for Truth and Freedom, in this new Movement which she started among us in 1914. Indian politics was still marked by a great deal of confusion and timidity. The older and so-called "Moderate" leaders while loudly professing their allegiance to "British Rule," did not seem to have any clear idea as to how that "Rule" was to be reconciled to the fulfilment of their equally loud demand for "self-government." They had taken up the cry of "Colonial self-government." But "Colonial self-government" practically means "sovereign independence." It has been openly recognised, since some time past, by every school of British politicans that the Over-Seas Dominions of Great Britain practically represented so many sovereign states. This Colonial Relation involved no sort of subjection to the Mother Country except what was willingly rendered to her by her grown-up children. The Colonies had been deliberately left free to work and develop along their own lines. They are free to enact their own laws to raise their own revenues, to appoint their own executive, in a word to discharge all those functions in regard to the administration of their own countries, that are discharged by the British Cabinet and the British Parliament in regard to the administration of the United Kingdom. The only matter in regard to which they are subject to the British Parliament is that of "foreign policy." But the Colonies are free, even here, to enter into commercial treaties with other alien nations —a freedom the existence of which was recognised, however grudgingly it might be in the case of Canada a few years back, when that Dominion proposed to form a commercial alliance with the United States. And, indeed, if any Dominion should find it necessary, in its own interests, to form any political alliance also with any foreign power, it is very doubtful whether the British Parliament will question that right and thus provoke a quarrel with it. Colonial Self-Government amounts, thus, for all practical purposes, to sovereign independence. The nominal subjection of the colonies to the Mother Country, is prompted partly by sentimental considerations, and partly by the more solid consideratians of national self-interest. The colonies are largely, though not wholly, peopled by men of the British stock. They have the same traditions, the same history, the same language and literature as the Britisher. The Colonies have hitherto been protected from foreign invasion by the prestige of the Mother Country. They had no national army worth considering and no Navy of their own. The need for these also did not arise until recently, when the sudden emergence of Japan into the comity of great world-powers created this necessity in the case of Australia and New Zealand on the Eastern and of Canada on the Western Pacific. And all the colonies have therefore been building up their own Army and Navy since some years past. Before they have been able to fully do so,—and even after they have developed and trained and equipped their land-power and sea-power to the utmost possible limit— they will always be more or less dependant upon the Imperial Army and the Imperial Navy for their self-protection. These are the considerations of substantial national self-interest that lend strength to the original sentimental considerations which keep the Dominions and the Mother Country together, and prevent the operation of any separatist tendencies that may exist in the former. In the case of Canada, with a large population derived from the French stock and of South Africa which is ethnically more Boer than British, considerations of self-interest alone keep them within the Empire. But even these would fail to preserve the Imperial Union, if British statesmanship had not most scrupulously respected the practical sovereignty of the Dominions.

The cry of Colonial self-government for India ignored all these actualities of the Colonial relation. Community of race, language, traditions and history, and the common race-consciousness and race-pride which these help to develop, do not exist between India and Great Britain. The sentimental basis of the Colonial relation does not exist here. On the contrary, there is unmistakable racial conflicts and competitions, a silent but vital war of ideals and cultures, between these two countries. A real and permanent units between two such divergent countries and races or nationalities as India and Great Britain, is only possible if it becomes vital to their self-preservation and self-fulfilment. Instincts of self-preservation and self-fulfilment have worked up the union between Great Britain and Canada and South Africa. And until this consciousness of the mutual need of India and the British Empire for their respective preservation and self-realisation is awakened and strengthened on both sides, the so-called Colonial relation can never be really worked up between them. This consciousness had not been quickened in the earlier years of the last decade. The so-called Colonial ideal lacked, therefore, both reason and reality in these days. Colonial self-government was to our politicians, only a cover then for complete national independence.

Mr. Dadabhai Naoroji clearly recognised this. In the Congress of 1906 he, therefore, did not simply repeat the old terms "Colonial self-government" or "self-government within the Empire," but freed the political ideal of modern India from all confusion of words and thoughts, by declaring that what we want is :—

" Self-government as in the Colonies or in the United Kingdom,—in a word—Swaraj."

This historic pronouncement, however, lent fresh strength and inspiration to the ideal of national independence which had already seized the imagination of the country.

In fact, "Moderate" or "Extremist," there was really no difference between them in regard to this ideal of ultimate sovereign independence for their country. One class declared that this independence would be had as a free gift from the British rulers, while the other said that no nation received this supreme right of governing themselves from another and more powerful nation that held political overlordship over them; but both accepted sovereign independence as their ultimate goal. Even Mr. Gokhale frankly admitted, in his Allahabad speech, in 1907, that he would put no limit to the aspirations of his countrymen, and if he preached the ideal of Colonial self-government in preference to any others, it was because it was likely to be more readily understood by the British people, and consequently it made the course of constitutional agitation for the political advancement of the country, smoother.

This was the condition of political thought in the country during the first decade of the present century. The emphasis of all our political aspirations was, as I have, already said, unmistakably on sovereign independence. There was, consequently, no room for any permanent reconciliation between our highest National ideal and the British connection. No principle had as yet been fully discovered and preached upon which a reasonable synthesis could be worked between Indian Nationalism and British Imperialism; and oven no sense of any real need for such a synthesis existed then, on either side.

I think, we must thankfully acknowledge that the earliest indication of a possible line of compromise and reconciliation between the highest Nationalist ideal and the Imperial connection, came from Lord Hardinge. His Excellency's historic Despatch of August, 1911, revealed a new ground of reconciliation between Indian Nationalism and British Imperialism. The implications of that important document clearly were the gradual evolution of a federal constitution inside India,—a constitution that would convert the present British India into something like a United States of India, the different Provincial Administrations representing the State-governments, and the Government of India, the federal Government of the Indian Union. This line of evolution was not altogether unfamiliar even to the British Empire. For, the Australian Commonwealth the Dominion of Canada, and the South African Union were shaped more or less after this federal ideal. Lord Hardinge's evident objective was to develop this federalism in the Government of India, and thus having secured complete autonomy for this Government, in all matters of domestic policy and internal affairs, to raise it to a status of perfect equality with the other self-governing members of the Empire, and secure for India a place of honour and responsibility commensurate with her strength and resources, her man-power, and brain power in the coming Council of the Empire. The Despatch of August, 1911, though its obvious meaning was sought to be repudiated by Lord Crewe and the spokesmen of the Bureaucracy both in this country and in England, undoubtedly contained a clear indication of the principle and policy that would be able to successfully work out a reasonable and permanent reconciliation and synthesis between the forces of Nationalism and the requirements of Imperialism, in relation to this country.

Lord Hardinge knew, from personal experience, the inner currents of modern international politics, more intimately than, perhaps, any other living British statesman or politician. He had been in most intimate touch with all the Chancellories of Europe. The new diplomacy summed up in the policy of international *entente* is, practically, of his own creation. It was Lord Hardinge who had supplanted the ancient animosity between Great Britain and Russia that had dominated the former's Eastern policy from before the Crimean War, by the new *entente-cordiale,* to which the former owes her superior position in the present war. He it was who initiated this policy in relation to France, largely under the inspiration of the late King-Emperor. The objective of this policy was to gradually isolate Britain's newest and most formidable rival in the continent of Europe. Lord Hardinge also knew the inner trends of current Asiatic politics. He was, I think, more or less keenly conscious not only of the

Pan-Mongolian menace, but equally also of the Pan-Islamic danger. And he tried to study the Indian Problem in the light of all these factors of current world-politics. He, therefore, clearly saw that only way to perpetuate the British Connection in India was to gradually evolve a Free and Antonomous Federal Government in the country and having raised it, thus, to a status of equality with the self-governing Dominions of the Empire, to make it an equal co-partner in the great British Empire. To put any other interpretation upon Lord Hardinge's Despatch of August, 1911, would be to ignore his past acquisitions and repudiate his claims to that far-seeing statesmanship which even his enemies have not dared to deny him.

Mrs. Besant had been to England more than once during the years 1908 to 1913. The so-called " unrest in India" had been more or less agitating the public mind there during these days. Democratic opinion as distinguised from the official Liberalism of Lord Morley and his colleagues in the Asquith Government, had been slowly " sensing" the need of doing some thing to satisfy Indian aspirations and offering some sort of a reasonable reconciliation between the people and the Government, who were clearly in a state of incipient war with each other. Lord Morley had tried his "Reforms," but these had failed to affect the "Unrest." Lord Minto had applied rigorous repressions; these too had failed. Sane opinion in England was therefore clearly in favour of some more radical remedy for the cure of this unrest in India. There were many people who were inclined to adopt a more conciliatory policy and grant a much larger measure of popular freedom to India than what the official Liberals were prepared to accept. Mrs. Besant saw all this. She lectured on the situation in India to influential gatherings of her old friends of the Fabian Society. In these addresses she took up a decidedly more liberal and sympathetic attitude towards the Unrest in India than she had taken in this country. And all these were indications of a change that was slowly coming over her in the matter of our present political life and struggles. She did not turn, therefore, suddenly, and by a long jump as it were, from a stern, if not actually an unfriendly, critic of the Nationalist Movement in India which was then practically vocal in Bengal only, into an ardent apostle of it. There has been a slow evolutionary process here, as in other departments of her ideas and activities.

The publication of Lord Hardinge's Despatch and the Repeal of the Curzonian Partition of Bengal, had been slowly helping the growth of a new school of political thought in the country, which was silently bringing the older parties—the Moderates and the Extremists—into line with each other. The earlier cry of "Colonial Self-Government" and "Self-Government within the Empire," though not wholly abandoned or openly repudiated was, all the same, being slowly supplanted by the new cry of "Equal Partnership or Co-Partnership in the Empire;" and, what was far more significant, the older avowal of "loyalty to British Rule" was silently giving place to the new "allegiance to the British Connection." All these were indications of the awakening of a new consciousness in the thought-leaders of the country —namely, the consciousness of India's need of the Imperial Connection in the interest as much of her own self-preservation, and self-fulfilment, as in those of the British Empire as well. India was no longer a suppliant for freedom and equality before the Empire. She claimed it for the preservation of the Empire itself, no less than for her own highest National self-fulfilment. She commenced to faintly recognise also the need of this Indo-British Federation for the preservation and promotion of universal world-peace.

This was the state of political thought in the country, when Mrs. Besant threw herself, for the first time, openly into our political activities. Coming back from her last visit to England, in the autumn of 1913, she saw the light of this new idea struggling to find fuller expresssion among us. It had as yet no organ of its own to make it vocal; no organisation to educate and train the people into this new Ideal of Nationalist Imperialism, as Mr. W. T. Stead had christened it, as early as 1911. It was still a very feeble cry in the land, a cry almost in the wilderness; and though the so-called "moderates" seemed to discover in it a consistent philosophy of their own inchoate and incoherent political thought, the so-called "extremists," wedded from their very birth to the ideal of sovereign and isolated independence, and particularly the extremist revolutionary wing of this school, looked askance at this new ideal, viewing it almost as unreal, if not dishonest, as the older "moderate" —cry of Colonial self-government. Both these schools had therefore, to be equally educated in the new Idea. Above all it was necessary that both should be led to recognice in it a complete reconciliation of all their earlier conflicts. Systematic and vigorous propagandist work was urgently wanted to effect this reconciliation between the schools of Indian politics on the one side, and between Indian Nationalism and the British Empire on the other.

"COMMONWEAL" AND "NEW INDIA"

With this object in view, Mrs. Besant first started her weekly organ, the "Commonweal" in January, 1914. One of the objects of this paper was, as she declared, "to draw Great Britain and India together, by making known in Great Britain something of Indian movement and of the *men who will influence from here the destinies of the Empire*." The italics are mine; and these words are a proof of the intuition of the writer regarding the future place of this country in the evolution of the British Empire.

But a weekly organ was hardly sufficient to keep pace with the growing needs of this new Nationalist Imperialist propaganda. Mrs. Besant, therefore, bought up the "Madras Standard" in July, 1914, and in a few days rechristened it, "New India." Indicating the policy of her Daily, Mrs. Besant who became the editor of both the papers—wrote :—

> "In politics, the paper will seek to embody the ideal of self-government for India along Colonial lines, remembering that the mission of every man and institution in this country is to bring about the speedy attainment of the triumph for which the Indian National Congress has steadily striven—Government by the inhabitants of India, for Indians, but under the educative guidance and control of British statesmanship until Colonial autonomy is attained."

In one matter, however, this new daily, repudiated from the very beginning, this "guidance and control of British statesmanship"—as offered through the Minto-Morley reforms of 1910. It declared that one of its cherished aims would be obliteration of all racial privileges and :—

> "The promotion of healthy co-operation and of the feeling of comradeship and solidarity between the various Indian peoples.

THE INDIAN NATIONAL CONGRESS

In keeping to the older phraseology of the Congress—Self-

Government on Colonial lines — Mrs. Besant was, evidently, moved by considerations of practical statesmanship. She saw that she must carry the Congress, the only living and active political organisation in the country—with her, in her new Nationalist propaganda, if it is to attain its object of uniting Indian opinon and bringing it to bear upon the course of Indian and Imperial policy. The Nationalists had been more or less discredited through the activities of the revolutionary party. The party or whatever of a party there had ever been, had been completely broken up, owing to the incarceration of Mr. Tilak and the enforced or voluntary exile of others who had represented it in 1906, '7 and '8. There was no possibility of reviving or reorganising it under existing conditions. The whole Nationalist Movement was under the ban of official displeasure. The Congress was recognised as sober and loyal by the authorities. It had the ear of the British public. Leaders of the Congress had been drafted into the new positions of trust and responsibility opened under the "Minto-Morley Reforms." Mrs. Besant's long experience of English political life, naturally, pointed to the Congress, therefore, as the best, if not, indeed, the only possible instrument for working out her plans.

TOWARDS A UNITED CONGRESS

Mrs. Besant had scrupulously kept away from the Congress. The Madras Congress of 1914 saw her, I think, for the first time, on the platform of the great National Assembly. But, one party, perhaps the most virile, and not less far-seeing than any others, was still out of it. The breach caused at Surat had not yet been re-covered. And she saw that the fight for India's freedom would never gain all the strength and inspiration it wanted for the attainment of its goal, unless we had a United Congress. Her first efforts, were, therefore, directed towards this end. The release of Mr. Tilak had put new life into the political activities of Maharastra. The Bombay Nationalists were willing to rejoin the Congress, if some honourable compromise could be worked up. Mrs. Besant offered her services to work this up. But personal animosities once aroused are exceedingly difficult to overcome. She did not, therefore, find it easy to bring about a reconciliation in time for the re-union of the rival parties at the Madras Congress of 1914. It will serve no useful purpose to rake up that old story. But though she failed in her main object of re-uniting the Congress that year, Mrs. Besant helped very materially to bring the so-called "Moderate" and "Extremist" political thought into line, by vigorously pushing forward the new Ideal of National Autonomy inside the coming Federation of the Empire.

This federal idea was in the air. For months before the meeting of the Congress (1914), the public press in the country, and particularly in Bengal, had been putting forward this ideal with great power and insistence. Not British Rule, but British Connection: not even Colonial Self-Government, but "equal co-partnership:" these were the new cry. Babu Bhupendra Nath Basu, who presided over this session of the Congress, declared that — "Neither subordination nor separation was wanted, but a joint partnership on equal terms." The constitution for India should be modelled on that of the United States of America or the Commonwealth of Australia, modified to suit India, and with a representative of the Crown at its head.

For the first time, Mrs. Besant spoke from our Congress platform, at this Madras session of 1914. She moved the Resolution relating to the position of Indians in the British Colonies, which welcomed Lord Hardinge's suggestion "of Reciprocity as the underlying basis of negotiations with the Colonies." In doing so, she declared:—

> "India claims the right, as a Nation, to justice among the Peoples of the Empire. India asked for this before the War. India asks for it during the War. India will ask for it after the War, but not as a reward but as a right does she ask for it. On that there must be no mistake."

She then asked them not to try to limit the right of the Colonies to be masters in their own houses, for India would have the same right soon. Whatever rule a Colony made as to the entry of Indians, that rule should India make as to the entry into India of the people of that Colony. She concluded with these words:—

> "India is growing in the sense of her own dignity. She is not content to be any longer a child in the nursery of the Empire. She is showing the responsibility of the man in Europe. Give her the freedom of the man in India."

In moving the Self-Government Resolution Babu Surendra Nath Banerjee, clearly foreshadowed the Home Rule Ideal, which Mrs. Besant commenced to preach almost immediately after the close of this Madras session. Babu Surendra Nath took his stand—

> "On the Proclamation of 1858, and called on the Government to give effect to the Despatch of August 25th, 1911, until "India would consist of a number of administrations, autonomous in all provincial affairs, with the Government of India above them, and possessing powers to interfere in case of mis-government." Mr. Banerjee quoted a letter from the Chairman of an English organisation for the introduction of a federal system of Government, in which he asked "India to organise her strength for this movement, and educate her public both in India, and all parts of the world." Babu Surendra Nath urged his audience to "formulate your scheme, press it upon the attention of the British public, and I am confident that your appeal will not fall upon heedless ears."

Her British instincts and long training in the methods of political work and progress in England, naturally led Mrs. Besant to proceed, in the formulation of this Home Rule Ideal, upon old precedent. It is, therefore, that she took up, as we have seen, the older Congress cry of Colonial Self-Government, as the first plank of her platfrom. In laying down the policy of her Daily paper,—*New India* :—she had spoken of the "speedy attainment" of the political Ideal of New India—*i.e.* "Government by the inhabitants of India for Indians," joined to the condition that this must be achieved—"under the educative guidance and control of British statesmanship." But she was soon forced by existing actualities to declare:—

> "That India welcomes English co-operation, but is getting very tired of English domination; that she is determined to get rid of coercive legislation, and to enjoy Self-Government. That she earnestly desires to have it with English help, but is resolved to have it."

And she added, not without a touch of bitterness, which was all-but-universally shared by the vast majority of our English-educated country-men,—

> "That she is perfectly well-aware that England did not "conquer India by the sword," but by the help of her own swords, by bribery, intrigue, and most acute diplomacy, fomenting of divisions, and playing of one party against another. But she is willing to let by-gones be by-gones, if Britain will now treat her on equal terms, and welcome her as a partner, not a dependent."

When laying down the policy of *New India,* Mrs. Besant was still more or less of an outsider to our actual political life, an ardent worshipper of the "Mother," but still a "worshipper at the gate." But in less than a year's time, coming into the very mid-currents of our political life and activities, she was forced to realise the cruel actualities of our situation. She saw that large numbers of our leading; political workers were still living under the old spell which the Bureaucracy had thrown over them either from honest conviction or from diplomatic motives, and they were preaching the old idea of receiving the political freedom of their country, as a free gift from their British masters, when they proved their fitness for it. Mrs. Besant saw that the very first condition of the success of political agitation in India was to remove this strange hallucination. India's Freedom must be wrought by India's own children. And the first step towards it, must be the quickening of a strong national self-consciousness in the country. For more than a century past, educated Indians had been taught to believe that they were incapable of any high achievement; that they lacked education and everything else that constitute the foundations of free political life; and that their salvation must come from their present British masters. All these notions had first to be corrected and removed, before any real and virile national self-consciousness could be awakened. This is why in all her earlier propagandist work in favour of Home Rule, Mrs. Besant laid so much emphasis on the past achievements of India, and the great capacities of the people which the benign Government of Great Britain had almost completely killed. This is the inner psychology of the powerful indictment which she brought against British rule in India, in the closing section of the "Historical Introduction" to the story of the Indian National Congress, as summarised and published by her, under the title of "How India Wrought for Freedom." The world had hitherto been told of the great good that the British have dona to India. The Indians themselves had been led to measure the benefits of this rule, by the courts of justice, the schools and colleges the railroads and canals, and other instruments of modern civilised life and administration which their present masters have established in the country but they had forgotten their own past. Mrs. Besant called up that past before them. In doing so, she pointed out how-India had in that past, autonomous and self-contained village communities and council-government; and how these have been replaced by "a hybrid system of Boards and Councils which are impotent for good," because these seek "to impose English methods on an ancient land which has its own traditions." She showed how "India's finest arts and industries" have been destroyed, through "the importation of cheap foreign goods." She similarly referred to India's ancient systems of irrigation and village sanitation and how these have been neglected in modern times. Finally she pointed out how the British Administration of India was "extremely costly," owing to the employment of Europeans "in the highest posts at the highest salaries." And India desires Home Rule, because—

> "she would do away with all this; would open everything to Indians—as indeed the Proclamation of 1858 promised—and require no foreign degrees as credentials; would abolish the India

Council; would acknowledge outside India, the authority only of the Crown and the Imperial Parliament, in which she enjoyed adequate representation. She would have her own Army and Navy, for protection and Imperial needs, not to hold her people down."

And finally she declared—

British rule has substituted coercion for improvements in Government, like any other autocracy. India would sweep all this coercive legislative away; she would not be afraid of her people possessing arms; she would not be afraid of the criticism of free speech and a free Press; she would reform abuses instead of strangling the expression of the discontent which abuses produce; she would emulate British rule in Britain, not British rule in India."

In a phrase:—India is enthralled, and she is determined to be free."

Frankly speaking, some of us specially in Bengal, did not quite like the repetition of these old indictments, by Mrs. Besant. We felt that the supreme need of the hour was to work up a reconciliation between Indian Nationalism and British Imperialism, and this re-iteration of our old grievances seemed to us rather likely to hinder than help this reconciliation. But we forgot that we had done this much-needed work already in Bengal, during the Swadeshi agitations of the last decade. Bengal had been completely disillusionised. Bengal had been fully initiated in the gospel of self-reliance and self-help. Old or young, no body in Bengal believed any more that the salvation of their country would come from the outside. The agitations of the last decade had fully awakened a keen and strong national self-consciousness in the Bengalee people. But it was not so in the rest of India. The destructive work that we had done in Bengal, had yet to be done in the other provinces. And it was, it seems to me, a recognition of this need which drove Mrs Besant to proclaim, in such strong language, the "other side" of the picture of British rule in India. It was necessary, not only for imparting-inspiration to India's fight for Home Rule, but also for creating those psychological conditions, without which no real and permanent reconciliation and synthesis could possibly be worked out between the legitimate demands of Indian Autonomy and the reasonable requirements of the Imperial Connection. For, no real and permanent synthesis becomes possible unless the antecedent antithesis are fully developed; and the imperious need for reconciliation and compromise never arises, as long as one party is weaker and less self-assertive than the other. Even in proclaiming these harsh, though not wholly untrue, indictments against British rule in India, Mrs. Besant was, therefore, working not really to cause a conflict between the Government and the people, but only to force both parties to a timely and friendly compromise and reconciliation, which is so essential for the good of India and the preservation of the Empire.

THE CONGRESS-COMPROMISE

But, for the success of her plan and policy, it was equally, if not even more, necessary that the articulate masses of India must demand this Home Rule with one united voice; and for this reason, the two great political parties or schools of thought, must be brought together under the banner of the old National Assembly. Throughout the year 1915, Mrs. Besant worked hard for this. In 1914, at the Madras session, Mrs. Besant had tried to get Art. XX of the Constitution of the Congress, which deals with the right of electing delegates, amended, to make it possible for those who had held aloof from the Congress, since the Convention of 1908, that adopted its present Constitution to rejoin it. But the consideration of her proposals was postponed to the next Congress (1915), a Committee being appointed in the meantime to consider and report upon these. This Committee, however, rejected Mrs. Besant's amendments, which, therefore, automatically fell through. But her efforts were not wholly fruitless. For, the Congress of 1914, did adopt an amendment of the Constitution, granting the right of election of Congress delegates, to "public meetings convened under the auspices of any Association which is of not less than two years' standing on the 31st December, 1915, and which has as one of its objects the attainment of Self-Government by India on Colonial lines within the British Empire by constitutional means." It was, this amendment of the Congress Constitution, which made it possible for the Nationalists to come back to the old organisation. And we owe this union of the two Parties more to the exertions and influence of Mrs. Besant than to any one else.

IN THE BOMBAY CONGRESS (1915)

But while exerting all her influence to bring back the large body of Nationalists who had been compelled to keep away from the

Congress since 1908, Mrs. Besant was actively engaged in laying the foundations of her Home Rule Movement. For this purpose she went about the principal centres of political activity in the country, delivering stirring addresses to crowded audiances, on the necessity of securing Home Rule for India. But though a very large and influential body of public opinion was thus created in favour of it, Mrs. Besant was anxious that this Home Rule Ideal should be accepted by the Congress, and the propaganda work in its behalf which the situation called for, should either be directly undertaken by the Congress itself or should be done, in any case, under the authority of that National organisation. When the Congress met, therefore, in Bombay in December 1915, Mrs. Besant convened a conference of all the leading sympathisers and advocates of Home Rule, for deciding the plan of operation. All the provinces were very largely represented at this Conference, which met a few hours before the opening of the Congress; and though the feeling was very strong that an All-India Home Rule League should be immediately started, Mrs. Besant counselled patience and led the meeting to put off the inauguration of the proposed League, to allow the Congress an opportunity of taking up the work itself. The principal interest in the Bombay Congress thus centred upon this question; and it may well be described as a "Preliminary Home Rule Congress;" for while practically accepting the scheme of Home Rule work presented by Mrs. Besant, the Subjects Committee asked for time to mature the plan of operation Mrs. Besant accepted this proposal, and, much to the disappointment, and even strong discontent of good many staunch Home-Rulers who had gone to Bombay especially for the Home Rule Conference, she agreed not to start her Home Rule organisation before September, 1916, which was the time-limit wanted by the Congress Executive to make their final decision. When, however, they failed to do anything in the matter, Mrs. Besant started her Home Rule League, as an independent-organisation which spread like almost wild fire from district to district, particularly in the Madras Presidency; while in Bombay the Nationalist party, under the leadership of Mr. Tilak, started a sister organisation, the Maharastra Home -Rule League, which too commenced to spread its branches all over that Province.

But though not formally accepting the Home Rule name, or the Home Rule propaganda, the Bombay session of the Congress in 1915, made a very distinct advance towards the Home Rule ideal, in a variety of ways. In the first place, the Presidential Address,—though pleading for delay—an appeal which was immediately repudiated by the majority of the Indian Press—distinctly reiterated the demand for "government of the people, for the people, *by the people*;" and it is significant that Sir S. P. Sinha put the last phrase in italics, thus showing the absolute unity of his ideal with that of the Home-Rulers. But notwithstanding, the extreme caution with which Sir S. P. Sinha presented this ideal the Congress of 1915 made a very marked advance in the formal presentation of the national demand for "responsible self-government."

The previous session of the Congress which met in December, 1914, at Madras, had passed the following Resolution under the heading of "self-government."

> "That in view of the profound and avowed loyalty that the people of India have manifested in the present crisis this Congress appeals to the Government to deepen and perpetuate it, and make it an enduring and valuable asset of the Empire, by removing all inviduous distinctions here, and abroad between His Majesty's Indian, and other subjects, by redeeming the pledges of Provincial Autonomy contained in the Despatch of the- 25th August, 1911, and by taking such measures as may be necessary for the recognition of India as a component part of a federated Empire, in the free and full enjoyment of the rights belonging to that status."

But the next session in Bombay (1915) made this demand more definite, and asked that the people of the country should be given "an effective control" over their Government; and. as definite steps towards securing this effective control, the Congress demanded, among others the following reforms :—

(a) The introduction of Provincial Autonomy including financial independence;

(b) Expansion and reform of the Legislative Councils so as to make them truly and adequately representative of all sections of the people and to give them an effective control over the acts of the Executive Government.

Instead of simply formulating these general principles, this Congress took very definite steps by authorising its executive, the

All-India Congress Committee, to "frame a scheme of reform and a programme of continuous work, educative and propagandist," embodying these principles and directed towards their popularisation. And Mrs. Besant helped very materially in the framing of this Resolution, which may, indeed, be said to have been largely her own handi-work. This Resolution of the Congress, it will be seen, practically accepted the whole programme of Home Rule initiated by her.

Mrs. Besant seconded this Resolution, and in doing so rightly characterised it as "perhaps the most momentous that had ever been laid before the National Congress during the thirty years of its splendid existence."

> "For, not only does it proclaim the steps to be taken towards the attainment of self-government, but also it lays down principles of reform, which, if they are embodied in the Committee's report, will make self-government a reality not in the distant vista of time, but within the life-time of the present generation, *(applause)* for, I find the bold demand is made that we should have an expansion and reform of the Legislative Councils so as to make them truly and adequately representative of all sections of the people; and most vital of all to give them an effective control over the acts of the Executive Government. Now, if adequate representation is given, if effective control over the acts of the Executive is granted, then it will be difficult to say that you have not got self-government in India. It is the largest step the Congress has ever taken, and it will make the Congress memorable in the gratful memory of the India of the future. Not only so, but - there is the vital proviso that the All-India Congress Committee is to frame not only a scheme of reform but a programme of continuous work, (hear, hear), educative and propagandist (hear, hear); not agitation, you must understand, but education and propaganda."

She then went on to state her reasons in support of this Resolution. These reasons contain the central text of the propagandist work which she carried on last year, and which brought her into open conflict, with the Indian Bureaucracy. These reasons were three in number; first the need of legislation on certain points; second the economic condition of the country; and third, the historical justification for the granting of self-government to India. On the first point, she said:—

"There are certain things that press upon the nation which would be rapidly altered if we had a majority, an effective majority, in the Legislative Councils, and if, as I hope, they be wholly elected."

> "This Congress has been asking for 30 years for the separation of executive and judicial functions and has not gained it. But in the Indian States that separation is already made. Baroda has done it, Gwalior has done it, some of the smaller States already possess it. And when you have self-government, you will not ask for it for thirty years, but you will make it in your first year (applause). You have asked for panchayats. Well, Gwalior, Baroda, Dewas and Patiala and other States have already established those village Councils successfully, and yet in British India it is impossible to get them thoroughly on foot. You will sweep away that Arms Act, of which our President so pointedly complained; you will get rid of the Press Act, which we have already protested against: you will get rid of the Seditious Meetings Act; you will get rid of the power to intern without trial and to imprison without justification (applause); you will get rid of that shameful revival of the old Bourbon barbarism, the old Regulation (Regulation 3 of 1818) which exists only in India to-day among all civilised nations of the world. Those are some of the reasons why we demand legislative assemblies with a majority at least of the representatives of the people."

Dealing with the "economic reason," she repeated the story of Indian taxation and Indian poverty, citing Messrs. Gokhale, Naoroji, Wacha, and the late Lord Salisbury, in support of her contention that the present system was largely responsible for this poverty.

> "I find Sir William Hunter saying that more than 40 millions of the people are always on the verge of starvation. I find Sir Charles Elliot saying that half the population never know what it is to have a full meal. And these, sir, are not "impatient idealists." They are historians (applause) and practical politicians. You have to consider that poverty; you have to realise what it means; you have to know the agony of hunger; and then think, as Sir Charles Elliot declared, of 100 millions of the agricultural population who never have a full meal. Some amount of impatience is justifiable when the people are suffering to that horrible extent. For this I tell you : that my fear for India is not the passionate

> enthusiasm of misguided youths, but the spectre of hunger, the frightful spectre of coming bankruptcy, which means the most awful of revolutions, the revolution of starving people whom none can check or rein in, when once they despair of help, (applause.)

She dwealt, however, with her third or last reason—the historical — in fuller detail; and may well be quoted here in full.

> Five thousand years ago, this country was trading with Babylon, and 3,000 years before the Christ down to 1613 after Christ, there is no break in the commercial and in the industrial prosperity of India. 5,000 years of self-government behind you, "But there were wars, there were revolts." Read history before you speak too glibly about the disturbances in medieval and in ancient India; for if there were wars here, there were wars there. Akbar was reigning when Queen Elizabeth was on the throne, and Queen Elizabeth gave the first charter to trade in India. In the reign of James I the first trading company was allowed to establish itself in Surat along the western coast. Since that time, in England, one King was beheaded, a second King was driven out of the country, and two civil wars on behalf of the exiled Stuarts have taken place, I do not know whether your wars were so very much more mischievous than the wars that prevailed over the whole of Europe during those historical times (applause.)

For, after all, is it not true that village organisation went on through them all ? Is it not true that villages were left untouched, save when the Huns swept down with fire and sword ? Is it not on record that while the soldiers were fighting, ploughmen were ploughing the land within sight of the battling army ? I put this to you as a particular proposition : that the test of the goodness of a Government is the wealth and prosperity of the people. While India governed herself so long her people were so well fed that every country in Europe fought for the right to have a charter to trade with this country. Whatever faults might have defaced that system, to-day our President has told us, that India is the most poverty stricken country in the world. I put the two things before you as the answer to the statement that we are not fit for self-government. I submit that 5,000 years of success is greater than the theories of a few Englishmen who consider that Indians are not their equals. (applause). We are told in the words of

Mr. Edwin Bevan that India is a poor cripple with limbs broken, tissues lacerated, tied up in splints and bandages by the benevolent English physicians and she must not move lest the wounds should not heal. India is no sick woman. She is a giant who was asleep and who is now awake. (applause.)

Are you fit for self-government ? Are you not sure? Mr. Gokhale said—and he knew his people well,—he said that you are compelled to live in an atmosphere of inferiority that made the tallest of you bow your heads and that the greatest moral wrong done to India was that she had changed in character under the present method of Government. These men who are here, representatives of India from every part of the land, these men are not the children of savages emerging from barbarism needing to be trained in the elements of self-government by a western nation. They are the children of heroes, the children of warriors, worthy to govern their own land,—(applause)—save for one reason : and that is that the very noblest among you seems to think himself inferior to the English men around you, Oh, if only you would trust yourselves, if only you would believe in your own power (hear, hear,) in your own strength and your own knowledge (applause.) If Sir Satyandra can tell us that he stood face to face with the Viceroy, has been an equal man in the Viceroy's Council, can we say that an Indian is not worthy to rule in his own land? Are we to think that he is the one swallow that does not make a summer ? Are we not to believe, as I believe, Sir, that there are hundreds like you (applause) who would show your own ability if they had a chance to do so ?

It was for preaching these ideas that her paper "New India" was first called upon to deposit a security of Rs. 2,000 in May, 1916, which was forfeited and a second security of Rs. 10,000 was demanded and paid. In July, 1916 the Defence of India Act was invoked by the Government of Bombay to prevent her from entering or residing in that Presidency. In September, the Chief Commissioner of the Central Provinces passed a similar order of prohibition on her. And all this was done, as we learnt from the reply given to a question on this subject put in the Viceroy's Council by the Hon. Mr. Kamini Kumar Chanda, with the previous knowledge of the Government of India.

THE LUCKNOW CONGRESS (1916) AND AFTER

But while the Executive was persecuting Mrs. Besant in various ways, the Home Rule propaganda was spreading far and wide, and when all political parties assembled in the United Congress at Lucknow last Christmas, Mrs. Besant was almost unanimously accepted as one of the most influential leaders of the new political life and thought in the country. The Lucknow Congress was practically a Home Rule Congress. The one Resolution which received the greatest attention from the Subjects' Committee and evoked the wildest enthusiasm in the Congress, was that on Self-Government. The word Home Rule was not used in the records of the Congress, but in demanding responsible self-government for the people of India, and asking for the introduction of the "scheme" prepared by the joint Committee of the Congress and the Moslem League, immediately after the war, as a clear and practical advance towards (his self-government, the Congress at Lucknow unanimously put its seal upon the Home Rule Movement. It further recognised the Home Rule Leagues as a part of itself, by calling upon them along with the Congress Committees, to carry on the educative and propaganda work of the Congress.

In seconding the Self-Government Resolution at Lucknow, she said :—

> "England is fighting for life, and has called India to help her with as much as India is able to give. Oh ! India would have given so much more, so many more men, so many more volunteers in order to help England in the day of her need. But England at her peril calls on Indian soldiers to fight the liberty of Belgium and the sacredness of treaties, and then sends those soldiers back home to find their people still in bondage and treaties disregarded, torn in pieces and thrown aside. That which England fights for in Europe she must admit here. There is only one thing which makes a Nation fit for freedom, and that is the heart to aspire after it, and the will which is determined to have it. England will not give you freedom, but England will pass an Apt of Parliament establishing freedom when she realises that you are in earnest, that you are tired of being played with, that you are determined to be free, and India's loyalty rests on a belief in the old England

and not in the English Bureaucracy, and her loyalty is the reasoned loyalty of freemen; she has asked for her place in the Empire, and until that is granted, there will be danger in the path of progress."

The next six months found her actively engaged in the work which she and others were called upon to carry in furtherance of the educative propaganda of the Congress-League scheme. And it is for this that she has been deprived of her freedom and "interned" under a special law which was never meant to apply to cases like these, even if there were any real grounds of setting the machinery of law against her. And the nature of this application was fully revealed in the interview which she had with Lord Pentland, on the 16th of June, on the eve of her interment, which was published in the *Hindu* and the truth of which has not been denied as yet.

At the beginning His Excellency said: "I have come down from Ooty, Mrs. Besant, in order to show my great consideration for you, and to speak to you myself and give you opportunity for consideration."

I said, "What am I to consider ?"

He said, "That is for you to decide, Mrs. Besant."

I asked His Excellency for what reason I was about to be interned.

He said, "I cannot discuss that Mrs. Besant."

I said, "In the Supreme Council, Sir Reginald Craddock stated that no one was interned without a full statement of the offence for which he was interned, and without being given a full opportunity for explanation or defence. I did not think at the time that it was true because some of my own friends had gone and I knew that they had had no such opportunity. I am very grateful to your Excellency for proving it to be false."

His Excellency answered, "I cannot disscuss it, Mrs. Besant."

I said, "I can only act according to my conscience and leave the rest to God."

He replied, "We must all do that."

I added, "I have nothing to regret in anything I have written or in anything that I have said, and, unless your Excellency tells me what you wish me to consider, I am at a loss to know what to suggest."

He replied, “That is for you to consider, Mrs. Besant.”

I said, “I have heard it said that your Excellency was going to offer me the alternative of going to England.”

He answered, “ For the period of the war, I will give you a safe conduct to England to take you through.”

I replied, “I do not intend to go to England.” Again I said, “we all understaud from your Excellency’s speech that you object to the Congress programme, and that it is identical with the programme of the Home Rule League.”

He replied, “I cannot reopen the subject, Mrs. Besant.”

I added, “I think I should say to your Excellency that the Home Rule League is simply supporting the Congress programme.” (Here I read from the Congress programme.)

His Excellency said, “I don’t know what that is.”

I replied, “It is the Reform Resolution passed by the Congress.”

He said, “I have not seen it.”

I answered, “Your Excellency, this is the Indian National Congress.”

After a pause, I said, “ In your Excellency’s Press communique just issued, you have stated that deliberate appeals had been made to the young to join in an active political agitation. People consider that this is aimed at me, but it is the exact opposite of my printed and spoken statements.”

He answered, “I do not know anything about that, Mrs. Besant, it applies to whomsoever it would suit. You must understand, Mrs. Besant, that we shall stop all your activities.”

I said, “I suppose so. I think I ought to say to your Excellency that at the present time the Madras Presidency is absolutely quiet and untroubled. Your proposed action will turn it into a condition of turmoil like that of Bengal.”

He answered, “I cannot discuss that, Mrs. Besant.”

I said, “It seems to me that as Your Excellency has no proposal to make and I have none, that I am wasting your Excellency’s time. Will you permit me to take leave?”

I arose and he walked with me to the door and on his way, he said, “I wish you to consider, Mrs. Besant, that we cannot discriminate and the whole of your activities will be stopped." I said, "You have all the power and I am helpless, and you must do what you like. There is just one thing I should like to say to Your Excellency and that is that I believe you are striking the deadliest blow against the British Empire in India." Then as we neared the door, I said, "You will pardon my saying to Your Excellency that, as you are acting as the Governor, I have no personal feeling against Your Excellency."

LAST WORDS

But Mrs. Besant knew that she would have to submit to be forcibly silenced by the Government. She might protest against unjust and unjustifiable executive orders, but her respect for law and order was strong enough to protect her from any illegal or criminal act. She knew she would have to obey the order of the Government. But, she felt, all the same, the severity of the blow which the Government was determined to deal her. In a letter, "To My Brothers and Sisters in India"—published in "New India" on the 13th of June, three days before she was silenced, she wrote :—

> "My real public life dates from my first public lecture on "The Political Status of Women," for the Co-operative Institute in August, 1874.
>
> Since then my life has been given wholly to the service of the public, as I have seen service, so that the deprivation of the liberty to render service is the greatest loss that can befall me. I know that the selfish and the unpatriotic cannot realise this, but those who have a similar Dharma, they will understand. Apart from the joy of service, life has no attractions for me, save the happiness that flows from a few deep and personal attachments. To surrender liberty and touch with those I love is to me worse than death. But to live free and with them, a coward and dishonoured, a traitor to Dharma and to India, would be hell, I take the easier path."

And these words really sum up the whole spitrit of her life and activities, extending over forty years.

The time is not yet perhaps to pass her latest conflicts with the Government through the tests of historical criticism. The minds of both her friends and foes are much too unsettled to calmly consider her latest activities. I leave these to be judged by the future historian of the Nationalist Movement in India.

But whatever the judgment of history may be on particular departments of her activities, or on particular opinions and ideals she may have held, from time to time,—there is one thing, on which the verdict of friends and foes alike, must be unanimous, namely, that with all her limitations, Mrs. Besant has been the bravest and purest worker for the public good, in her generation, and that ever since she joined the public life, her one, persistent aim has been, to live

For overy cause that lacks assistance,
For every wrong that needs resistance,
For the future in the distant
And the good that she could do.

CORRECTIONS

SECTION:—

"The Evolution of Mrs. Besant's philosophy."

For—"the death of her only child."

Read—"The serious illness of her baby daughter."

NEXT SENTENCE:—

For "death" read "illness."

For "crushing" read "suffering."

NOTE:—

(a) The real philosophy of Mrs. Besant's revolt must be found in the popular Christian doctrine that death and disease came to this world as *punishment* of the *sin* of the First Parents.

(b) In the third para of this section—

Bead the following:— "Mrs. Besant's intellect is distinctly of this type etc." to "positive atheism."

This statement though verbally correct is not really true. Mrs. Besant while calling herself an "Atheist" did not actually *deny* the existence of God. She said that she could not *deny* that which she did not know.

II

SECTION:—

"Materialism and Occultism." Page 24, line 11-12—For "Isis unveiled" read "Secret Doctrine."

Page 24, Line 30-31. Read "Secret Doctrine" for "Isis unveiled."